A-Z DARLI

G000278588

CONTENTS

REFERENCE

Motorway	A1(M)	Car Park (Selected)	P
A Road	A1150	Church or Chapel	†
B Road	B6279	Fire Station	■
Proposed		Hospital	H
Dual Carriageway		Information Centre	i
One-way Street	→	National Grid Reference	⁴25
Traffic flow on A Roads is indicated by a heavy line on the driver's left.			
		Police Station	▲
Restricted Access		Post Office	★
Pedestrianized Road		Toilet	
Track & Footpath		without facilities for the Disabled	▽
Residential Walkway		with facilities for the Disabled	▽
Railway	Level Crossing / Station / Tunnel	Educational Establishment	
		Hospital or Hospice	
Built-up Area	DERBY ST	Industrial Building	
Local Authority Boundary	— · — · —	Leisure or Recreational Facility	
Posttown Boundary		Place of Interest	
Postcode Boundary (within Posttown)	— — — —	Public Building	
		Shopping Centre or Market	
Map Continuation	▲ 10	Other Selected Buildings	

Scale : 1:15,840   4 inches (10.16 cm) to 1 mile, 6.31 cm to 1 Kilometre

0	¼	½	¾	1 Mile

0	250	500	750 Metres	1 Kilometre

Copyright of Geographers' A-Z Map Company Ltd.

Fairfield Road, Borough Green, Sevenoaks, Kent TN15 8PP
Telephone : 01732 781000 (Enquiries & Trade Sales)
           01732 783422 (Retail Sales)

www.a-zmaps.co.uk

Ordnance Survey® This product includes mapping data licensed from Ordnance Survey® with the permission of the Controller of Her Majesty's Stationery Office.

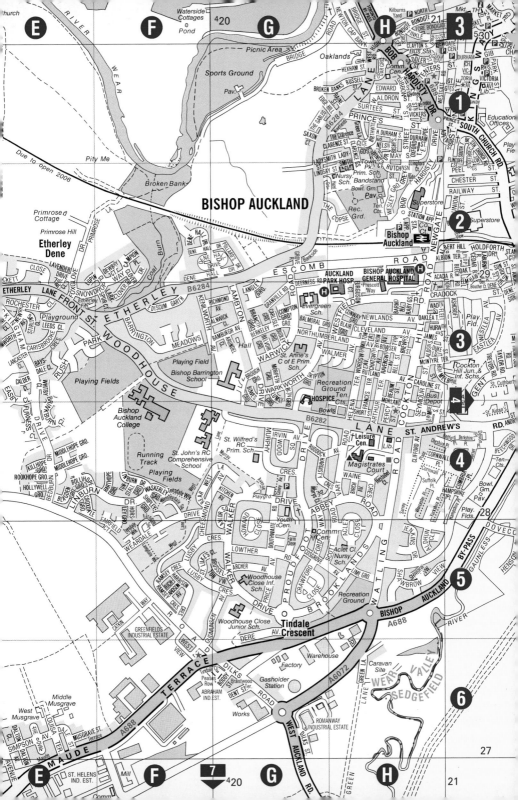

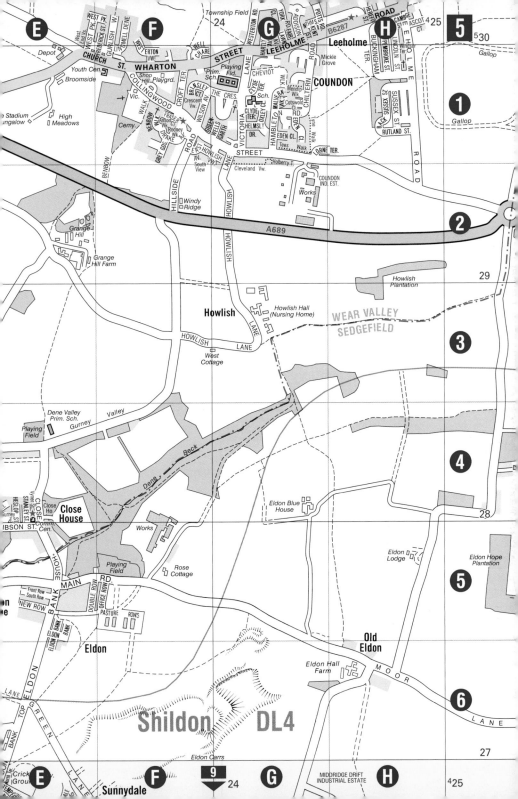

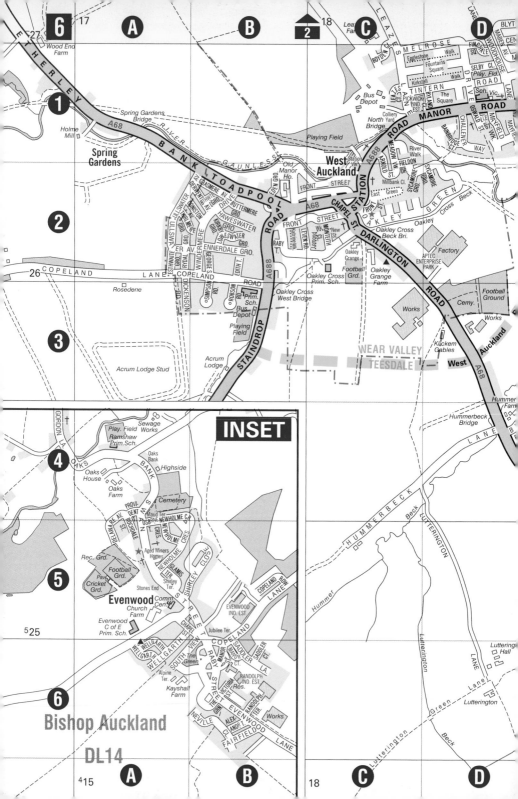

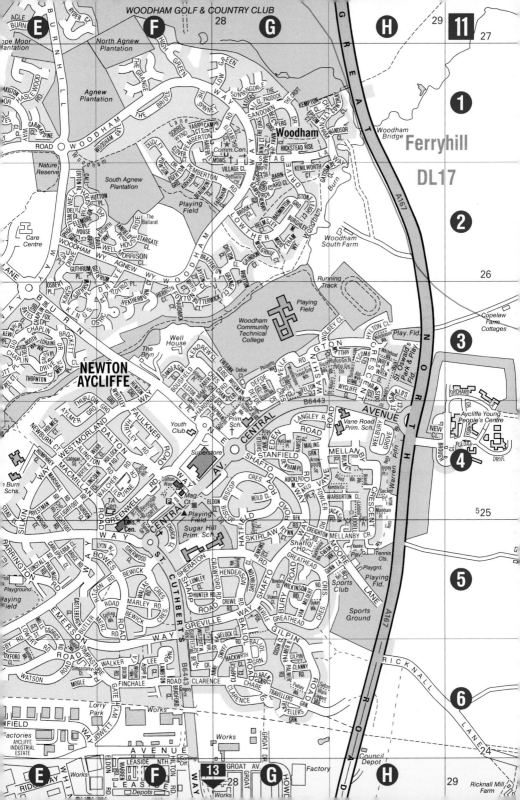

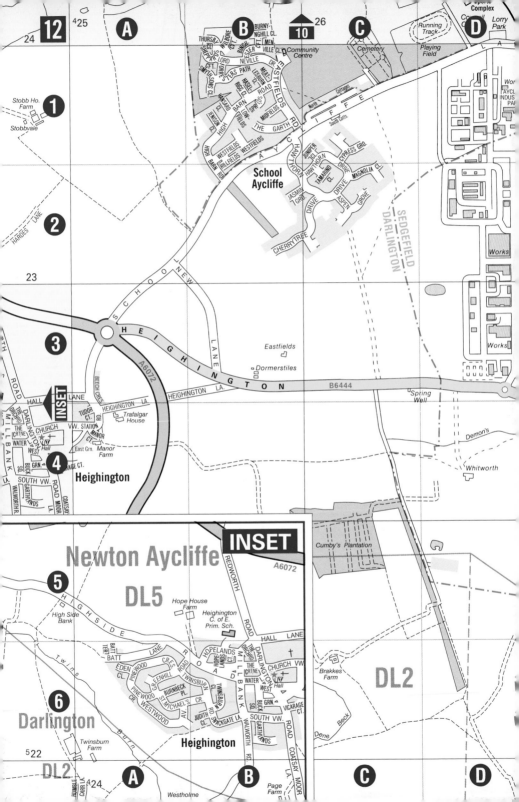

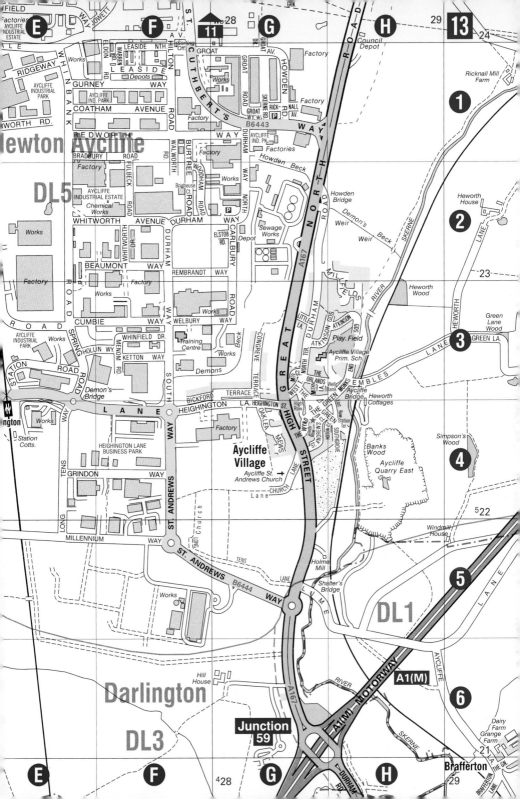

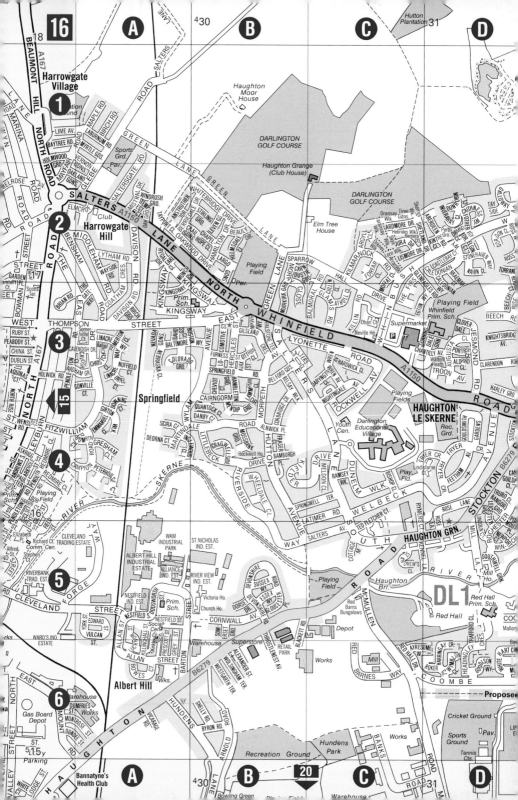

E · F · G · H

INSET

Darlington

DL2

Barmpton Grange Farm
Barmpton
Jasmine Cott.
Ellyhill Wood
Elly Hill House
Elly Hill
White se Farm
PTON M.
Burdon Gardens
Carcut Bridge

LANE
32

434

HILLHOUSE (ROMAN ROAD)

NORTON CRES.
NORTON DALE RD.
NORTON BACK LA.
ABBEY ROAD
STOCKTON ROAD
1
517
Play Area

Raby Farm
Goodwood CL.
Well House Farm
EAST CL.
Chapel Row
Stainton
South Vw.
Laurel Ter.
Hillside Ter.
Sadberge

DARLINGTON RD. WEST
ORCHARD
THE
CHURCH VW.
CHURCH LA.
BEACON GRANGE PK.
Hall
Beacon Grange Farm
Sadberge Reservoir (disused)
Subway
MIDDLETON ROAD
A66
Lea Close
2

BEACON HILL

Carcut Beck

3 INSET ▶

BEACON HILL

Mill Batts
Great Burdon
Cricket Grd.
The Green
STOCKTON RD.
BISHOPTON LANE
A1150
BUESS LANE
A66
Subway
Little Burdon
4

Great Burdon Bridge
Great Burdon Farm
RIVERSIDE DR.
TURNPIKE CL.
Chichester W.
WK.

Darlington

TOFT HILL
16

DL2
5

Ct.
Hickstead Ct.
Chepstow Ct.
Bisley Ct.
Twickenham Rd. DRIVE
Elland Ct.
Epsom Ct.
Aintree Ct.
Aviemore Ct.
Anfield Ct.
DRIVE
A66 LANE

6
Morton Palms
South Burden Farm
515

E · **21** ▼ · F · G · H

Reservoir 32
CLOSE
33

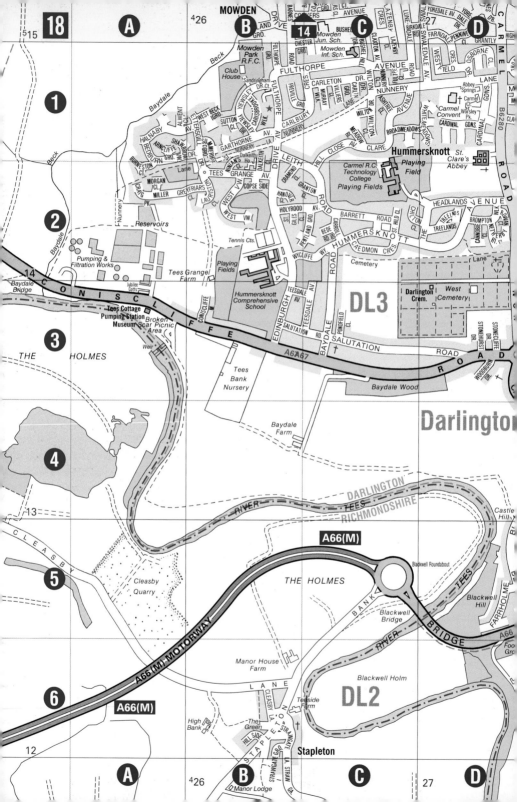

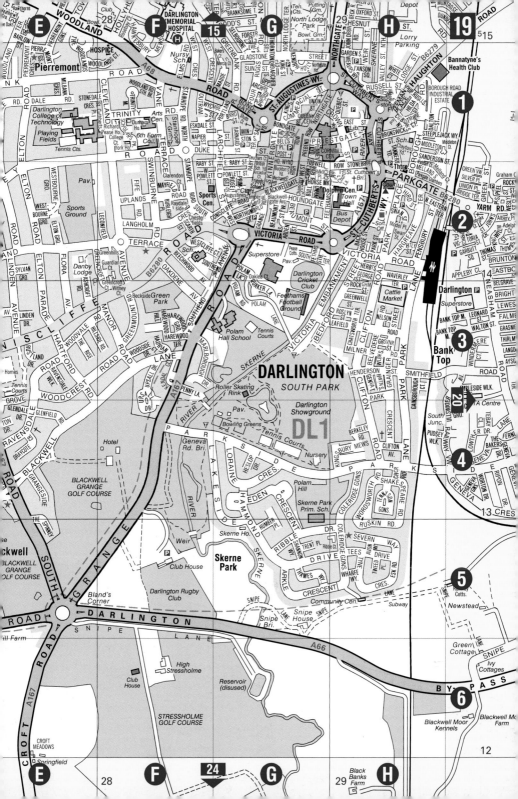

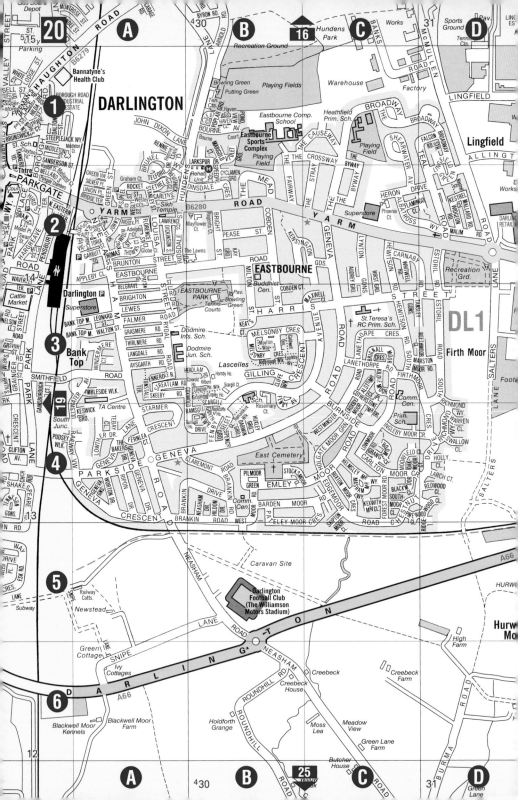

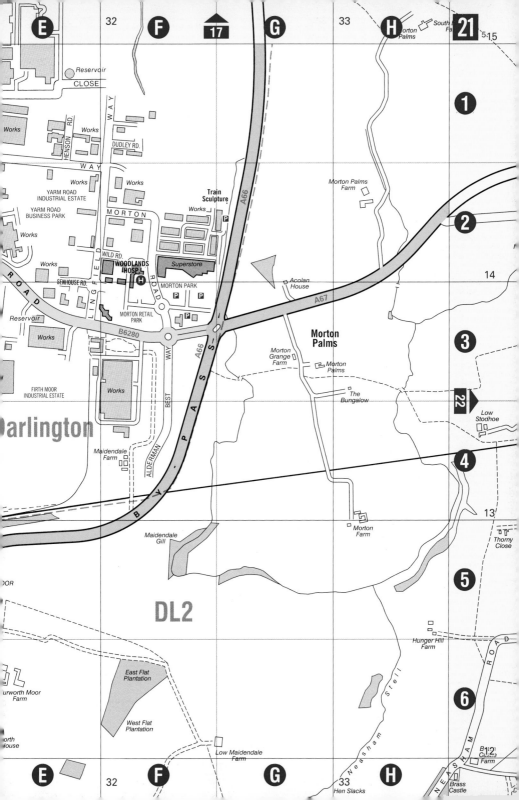

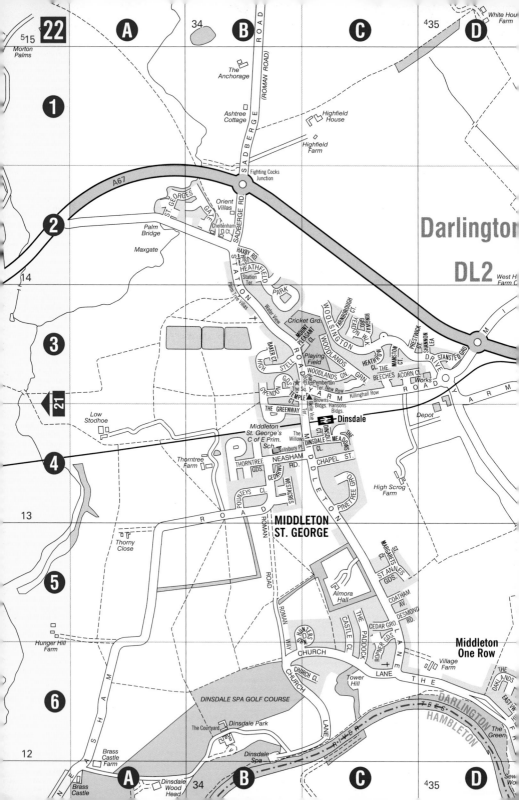

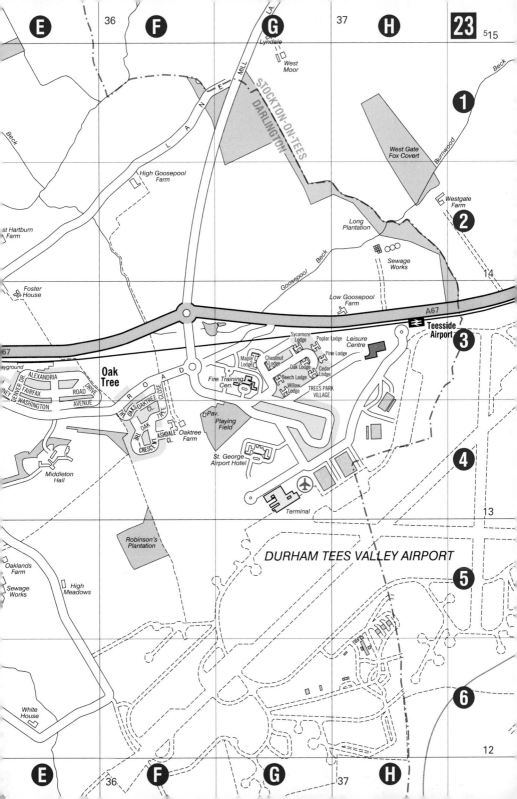

1

2

14

3

4

13

5

6

12

Beck

Mill La

Lyndale

West Moor

STOCKTON-ON-TEES

DARLINGTON

LANE

West Gate Fox Covert

Burnwood

Beck

High Goosepool Farm

Westgate Farm

st Hartburn Farm

Long Plantation

Goosepool Beck

Sewage Works

Foster House

Low Goosepool Farm

A67

Teesside Airport

A67

Oak Tree

Sycamore Lodge

Poplar Lodge

Leisure Centre

Maple Lodge

Chestnut Lodge

Pine Lodge

playground

ALEXANDRIA

DENVER DR.

FAIRFAX

NEY WASHINGTON

THE OAKS

OAKTREE CL.

OAKTREE CLOSE

ROAD

DRIVE

AVENUE

Oak Lodge

Beech Lodge

Cedar Lodge

Willow Lodge

TREES PARK VILLAGE

Fire Training Cen.

Pav.

THE OAK CRESC.

ASHDALE CL.

Oaktree Farm

Playing Field

St. George Airport Hotel

Middleton Hall

Terminal

Robinson's Plantation

Oaklands Farm

Sewage Works

High Meadows

DURHAM TEES VALLEY AIRPORT

White House

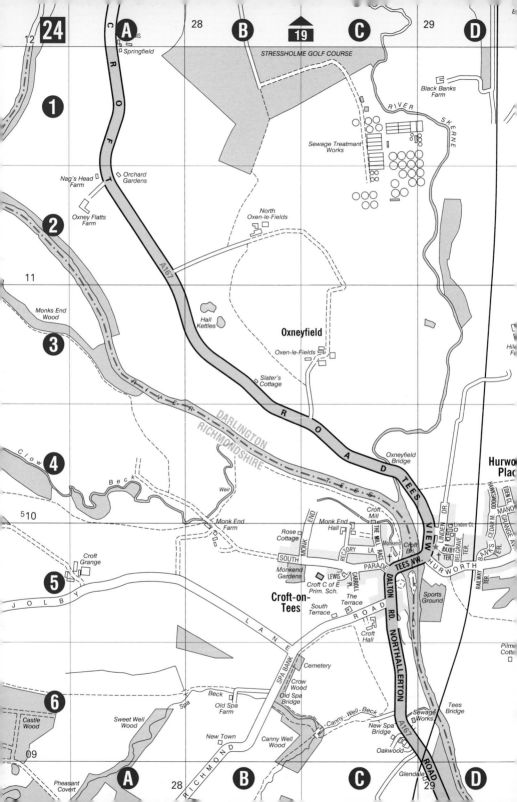

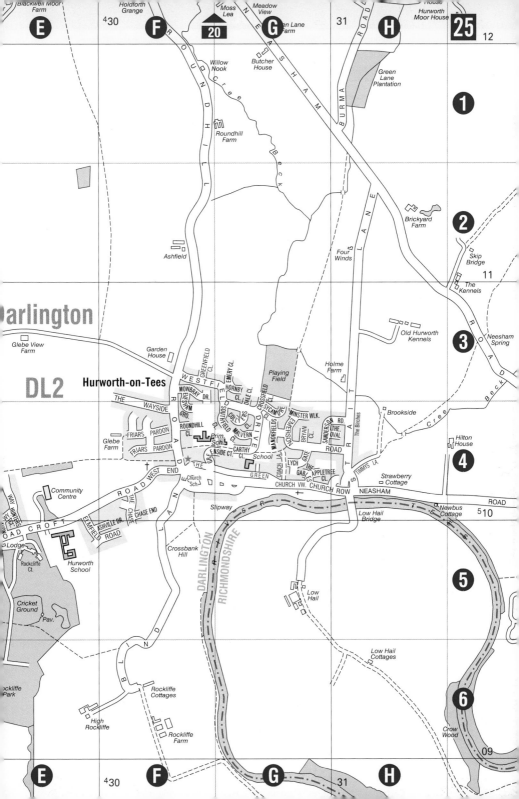

INDEX

Including Streets, Places & Areas, Hospitals & Hospices, Industrial Estates,
Selected Flats & Walkways, Stations and Selected Places of Interest.

HOW TO USE THIS INDEX

1. Each street name is followed by its Postcode District and then its Locality abbreviation(s) and then by its map reference;
e.g. **Adelaide Bank** DL4: Shil . . . .5C **4** is in the DL4 Postcode District and the Shildon Locality and is to be found in square 5C on page **4**.
The page number is shown in bold type.

2. A strict alphabetical order is followed in which Av., Rd., St., etc. (though abbreviated) are read in full and as part of the street name;
e.g. **Beck Rd.** appears after **Beckett Cl.** but before **Beckside**

3. Streets and a selection of flats and walkways too small to be shown on the maps, appear in the index with the thoroughfare to which it is connected
shown in brackets; e.g. **Ashfield Ct.** DL3: Darl . . . .1G **19** (off Larchfield St.)

4. Addresses that are in more than one part are referred to as not continuous.

5. Places and areas are shown in the index in **BLUE TYPE** and the map reference is to the actual map square in which the town centre or area is located
and not to the place name shown on the map; e.g. BISHOP AUCKLAND 1H **3**

6. An example of a selected place of interest is Darlington Railway Cen. & Mus. 5G 15

7. An example of a station is **Bishop Auckland Station (Rail)** 2H 3

9. An example of a hospital or hospice is AUCKLAND PARK HOSPITAL 3H 3

GENERAL ABBREVIATIONS

App. : Approach	**Cft.** : Croft	**Info.** : Information	**Rdbt.** : Roundabout
Arc. : Arcade	**Dr.** : Drive	**Junc.** : Junction	**Sth.** : South
Av. : Avenue	**E.** : East	**La.** : Lane	**Sq.** : Square
Bk. : Back	**Emb.** : Embankment	**Mkt.** : Market	**St.** : Street
Bldgs. : Buildings	**Ent.** : Enterprise	**Mdw.** : Meadow	**Ter.** : Terrace
Bungs. : Bungalows	**Est.** : Estate	**Mdws.** : Meadows	**Trad.** : Trading
Bus. : Business	**Fld.** : Field	**M.** : Mews	**Up.** : Upper
Cen. : Centre	**Gdns.** : Gardens	**Mt.** : Mount	**Vw.** : View
Chu. : Church	**Gth.** : Garth	**Mus.** : Museum	**Vs.** : Villas
Cl. : Close	**Ga.** : Gate	**Nth.** : North	**Wlk.** : Walk
Cnr. : Corner	**Grn.** : Green	**Pde.** : Parade	**W.** : West
Cott. : Cottage	**Gro.** : Grove	**Pk.** : Park	**Yd.** : Yard
Cotts. : Cottages	**Ho.** : House	**Pl.** : Place	
Ct. : Court	**Ho's.** : Houses	**Ri.** : Rise	
Cres. : Crescent	**Ind.** : Industrial	**Rd.** : Road	

LOCALITY ABBREVIATIONS

Auc P : **Auckland Park**	Darl : **Darlington**	Hur M : **Hurworth Moor**	Redw : **Redworth**
Ayc : **Aycliffe**	Eld : **Eldon**	Hurw : **Hurworth-on-Tees**	Rush : **Rusheyford**
Bam : **Barmpton**	Eld L : **Eldon Lane**	Hur P : **Hurworth Place**	Sadb : **Sadberge**
Bish A : **Bishop Auckland**	Esc : **Escomb**	Leeh : **Leeholme**	St H : **St Helen Auckland**
Braff : **Brafferton**	Ether D : **Etherley Dene**	Low E : **Low Etherley**	Sch A : **School Aycliffe**
Cleas : **Cleasby**	Ether G : **Etherley Grange**	Midd R : **Middleton One Row**	Shil : **Shildon**
Coat M : **Coatham Mundeville**	Even : **Evenwood**	Midd G : **Middleton St George**	Stap : **Stapleton**
Coun : **Coundon**	Even G : **Evenwood Gate**	Middr : **Middridge**	Toft H : **Toft Hill**
C'gate : **Coundongate**	Gt Bur : **Great Burdon**	Neas : **Neasham**	Tor : **Toronto**
Coun G : **Coundon Grange**	Haugh S : **Haughton-le-Skerne**	Newt A : **Newton Aycliffe**	W Auc : **West Auckland**
Croft T : **Croft-on-Tees**	Heigh : **Heighington**	Old E : **Old Eldon**	Wit P : **Witton Park**
Dalt T : **Dalton-on-Tees**	H Eth : **High Etherley**	Rams : **Ramshaw**	

A

	Aged Miners Homes	**Alderson St.** DL14: Bish A 3H 3	**Alston Moor Cl.** DL1: Darl 3C 20
	DL14: Even 5A 6	**Alderwood Cl.**	**Alston Wlk.** DL5: Newt A 4C 10
Abbey Rd. DL2: Sadb 2H 17	**Agnew Way** DL5: Newt A 2F 11	DL1: Haugh S 3D 16	**Alverton Dr.** DL3: Darl 2D 14
DL3: Darl 2D 18	**Agricola Ct.** DL3: Darl 2D 14	**Aldfrid Pl.** DL5: Newt A 3F 11	DL5: Newt A 2D 10
DL14: Bish A 4G 3	**Ainsley Gro.** DL3: Darl 2D 14	**Aldgrove Way** DL3: Darl 4F 15	**Alwent Cl.** DL3: Darl 1A 18
Abbey Springs DL3: Darl 1D 18	**Ainsty Hunt** DL5: Newt A 3B 10	**Aldhun Cl.** DL14: Bish A 5H 3	**Alwyn Rd.** DL3: Darl 1H 15
Abbotsfield Way DL3: Darl 2C 14	**Aintree Ct.** DL1: Darl 6E 17	**Aldwyn Wlk.** DL5: Newt A 3H 11	**Amberley Gro.** DL3: Darl 2C 14
Abercorn Ct. DL3: Darl 2C 14	**Airton Pl.** DL5: Newt A 4D 10	**Alexander St.** DL14: Bish A 5H 3	**Ambleside Wlk.** DL1: Darl 3A 20
Aberdeen Rd.	**Ajax St.** DL1: Haugh S 3B 16	**Alexander Ter.** DL14: Even 6B 6	**Amiens Cl.** DL3: Darl 4D 14
DL1: Haugh S 2D 16	**Albatross Way**	**Alexandra Gdns.** DL4: Shil 1E 9	**Ampleforth Way** DL3: Darl 5B 14
Abraham Ind. Est.	DL1: Darl 2C 20	**Alexandra St.** DL4: Shil 1E 9	**Anfield Ct.** DL1: Darl 6E 17
DL14: Bish A 6F 3	**ALBERT HILL** 6A 16	**Alexandria Dr.** DL2: Midd G . . .3E 23	**Angram Pl.** DL5: Newt A 4C 10
Acacia Rd. DL14: Bish A 2H 3	**Albert Hill** DL14: Newt A 2A 4	**Alfred St.** DL1: Darl 5H 15	**Annandale** DL1: Haugh S 2D 16
Acacia St. DL3: Darl 5F 15	**Albert Hill Ind. Est.**	**Alington Rd.** DL5: Newt A 4E 11	**Anne Swyft Rd.**
Acle Burn DL5: Newt A 1E 11	DL1: Darl 5A 16	**Allan St.** DL1: Darl 6A 16	DL5: Newt A 6G 11
Aclet Cl. DL14: Bish A 5H 3	**Albert Rd.** DL1: Darl 5H 15	**Allan Wlk.** DL5: Newt A 4G 11	**Ann's Ter.** DL3: Darl 5G 15
Acorn Cl. DL2: Midd G 3C 22	**Albert St.** DL1: Darl 2A 20	**Alliance Ind. Est.** DL1: Darl 5A 16	**Anson Wlk.** DL3: Coun 1F 5
Adamson St. DL4: Shil 4E 9	DL4: Shil 1E 9	**Alliance St.** DL3: Darl 5G 15	**Anstruther Dr.** DL1: Darl 2A 16
Addison Rd. DL14: Leeh 1G 5	**Albery Pl.** DL1: Darl 2A 20	**Allington Way** DL1: Darl 1D 20	**Appleby Cl.** DL1: Darl 2A 20
Addison St. DL14: Coun G 4D 4	**Albion Av.** DL4: Shil 1D 8	**All Saints Ind. Est.** DL4: Shil . . .4F 9	**Appleby St.** DL14: Bish A 4B 4
Adelaide Bank DL4: Shil 5C 4	**Albion Ter.** DL14: Bish A 2H 3	**All Saints Rd.** DL4: Shil 6E 9	**Appleton Cl.** DL3: Darl 4G 15
DL14: Bish A 5C 4	DL14: Wit P 1A 2	**Alma Rd.** DL4: Shil 3E 9	**Appletree Cl.** DL2: Hurw 4G 25
Adelaide St. DL1: Darl 2A 20	**Aldam St.** DL1: Darl 5H 15	**Almond Ct.** DL4: Shil 3F 9	**Aptec Ent. Pk.** DL14: W Auc 2D 6
DL3: Darl 5F 15	**Aldbrough Wlk.** DL1: Darl 3B 20	**Alnwick Cl.** DL14: Bish A 3G 3	**Aquinas Ct.** DL3: Darl 3H 15
DL4: Shil 3D 8	**Alderman Best Way**	**Alnwick Gro.** DL5: Newt A 2G 11	**Arcadia Ct.** DL3: Darl 2G 19
DL14: Bish A 1A 4	DL1: Darl 4F 21	**Alnwick Pl.** DL1: Haugh S 4B 16	**Archdeacon Cres.** DL3: Darl 5C 14
Adelaide Ter. DL4: Shil 6C 4	**Alderman Leach Dr.**	**Alpine Ter.** DL14: Even 6A 6	**ARCHDEACON NEWTON** 2A 14
Adelphi Ct. DL1: Darl 2A 20	DL3: Darl 3C 14	**Alston Cres.** DL5: Newt A 4C 10	**Archer Av.** DL14: Bish A 5G 3

Archer Rd.—Brook Cl.

Archer Rd. DL2: Midd R . . . 6D 22
Archer St. DL3: Darl . . . 1G 19
(not continuous)
Ardmore Dr. DL1: Haugh S . . . 2C 16
Argyll Cl. DL1: Haugh S . . . 2C 16
Arkendale St. DL1: Darl . . . 4H 15
Arkle Cres. DL1: Darl . . . 5G 19
Armstrong Cl. DL5: Newt A . . . 3H 11
Armstrong Ct. DL3: Darl . . . 5E 15
Arncliffe Gro. DL3: Darl . . . 1A 18
Arncliffe Pl. DL5: Newt A . . . 4E 11
Arnold Rd. DL1: Darl . . . 6B 16
Arnold St. DL14: W Auc . . . 1C 6
Arran Wlk. DL1: Haugh S . . . 2C 16
Arrowsmith Sq.
DL5: Newt A . . . 4G 11
Arthur St. DL3: Darl . . . 5G 15
DL14: Eld L . . . 5D 4
Arthur Ter. DL14: Bish A . . . 4H 3
Arundel Cl. DL14: Bish A . . . 3G 3
Arundel Dr. DL3: Darl . . . 4C 14
Ascot Ct. DL14: Leeh . . . 1H 5
Ascot Vw. DL1: Darl . . . 5D 16
Ashcroft Gdns.
DL14: Bish A . . . 3A 4
Ashcroft Rd. DL3: Darl . . . 3E 19
Ashdale Cl. DL2: Midd G . . . 4F 23
Ashfield DL5: Newt A . . . 5D 10
Ashfield Ct. *DL3: Darl . . . 1G 19*
(off Larchfield St.)
Ash Gro. DL4: Shil . . . 2E 9
Ash Tree Cl. DL5: Newt A . . . 2D 10
Ashtree Cl. DL3: Darl . . . 1C 18
Ashville Dr. DL2: Hurw . . . 5F 25
Askrigg Cl. DL5: Newt A . . . 3E 11
Askrigg St. DL1: Darl . . . 4H 15
Aspen Ct. DL4: Shil . . . 3F 9
Aspen Gro. DL5: Sch A . . . 2C 12
Association Ct. DL4: Shil . . . 1D 8
Association St. DL4: Shil . . . 1D 8
Aston Ter. DL3: Darl . . . 6D 14
Atherstone Way DL3: Darl . . . 4A 14
Atherton Ter. DL14: Bish A . . . 4C 4
Atholl Cl. DL1: Haugh S . . . 3C 16
Atkinson Gdns. DL5: Ayc . . . 3G 13
Auckland Av. DL3: Darl . . . 5D 14
Auckland M. DL5: Newt A . . . 4G 11
Auckland Oval DL3: Darl . . . 4E 15
AUCKLAND PARK . . . 3D 4
AUCKLAND PARK HOSPITAL . . . 3H 3
Auckland Pl. DL5: Newt A . . . 4G 11
Auckland Rd. DL14: Bish A . . . 4B 4
Auckland Ter. DL4: Shil . . . 1C 8
Auckland Vw. DL14: H Eth . . . 6B 2
Auckland Way DL14: Auc P . . . 2C 4
Auckland Wynd DL4: Shil . . . 1C 8
Audrey Gro. DL1: Darl . . . 2C 20
Augusta Cl. DL1: Haugh S . . . 3D 16
Aviemore Ct. DL1: Darl . . . 6E 17
Avon Ct. DL5: Newt A . . . 3D 10
Avon Rd. DL2: Hur P . . . 5E 25
Avon Way DL1: Darl . . . 5H 19
Aycliffe Ind. Est.
DL5: Newt A . . . 6E 11
(not continuous)
Aycliffe Ind. Pk.
DL5: Newt A . . . 1E 13
(not continuous)
Aycliffe La. DL1: Braff . . . 6H 13
AYCLIFFE VILLAGE . . . 4G 13
Aylmer Gro. DL5: Newt A . . . 4E 11
Ayresome Way DL1: Darl . . . 6C 16
Aysgarth Cl. DL5: Newt A . . . 4D 10
Aysgarth Rd. DL1: Darl . . . 3A 20
Ayton Dr. DL3: Darl . . . 4E 19

B

Bk. Cheapside DL4: Shil . . . 1E 9
Bk. Church St. *DL4: Shil . . . 1E 9*
(off Church St.)
DL14: Coun . . . 1F 5
(off Church St.)
Backhouse St. DL1: Darl . . . 2H 19
Backhouse Wlk.
DL5: Newt A . . . 5G 11
Back Sth. Chu. Rd.
DL14: Bish A . . . 1A 4
Back St. *DL3: Darl . . . 1F 19*
(off Duke St.)
Bk. Sussex St. DL14: Leeh . . . 1H 5
Badminton Cl. DL1: Darl . . . 5D 16
Badminton Gro.
DL5: Newt A . . . 2G 11
Bainbridge Ct. DL14: St H . . . 1D 6
Bakehouse Hill *DL1: Darl . . . 2G 19*
(off Tubwell Row)
DL14: Bish A . . . 1A 4
(off Market Pl., not continuous)
Bakers, The DL1: Darl . . . 4A 20
Bakers Ct. DL3: Darl . . . 1G 19
Bakewell M. DL3: Darl . . . 3C 14
Bakewell Pl. DL5: Newt A . . . 3E 11
Baliol Grn. DL5: Newt A . . . 6G 11
Baliol Rd. DL5: Newt A . . . 5G 11
Ballarat, The DL5: Newt A . . . 2F 11
Balliol Ct. DL1: Darl . . . 3A 16
Balmoral Gro. DL14: Bish A . . . 3G 3
Balmoral Rd. DL1: Haugh S . . . 3C 16
Baltic, The DL14: Wit P . . . 1A 2
Baltimore Way
DL1: Haugh S . . . 3A 16
Bamburgh Av. DL14: Bish A . . . 3G 3
Bamburgh Cres.
DL5: Newt A . . . 2G 11
Bamburgh Pl.
DL1: Haugh S . . . 4B 16
Bangor Gro. DL1: Haugh S . . . 4D 16
Banklands Ct. DL3: Darl . . . 5E 15
Banklands Rd. DL3: Darl . . . 5E 15
Bankside DL14: Bish A . . . 2G 3
Banks Rd. DL1: Darl . . . 6C 16
Banks Ter. DL2: Hur P . . . 5D 24
BANK TOP . . . 3H 19
Bank Top M. DL1: Darl . . . 3A 20
Bank Well DL14: Low E . . . 5B 2
Bankwell Dr. DL14: Low E . . . 5B 2
Bannatyne's Health Club . . . 1A 20
Barden Moor Rd. DL1: Darl . . . 4B 20
Barlow St. DL3: Darl . . . 6E 15
BARMPTON . . . 1E 17
Barmpton La.
DL1: Bam, Haugh S . . . 3D 16
Barmpton M. DL1: Haugh S . . . 2E 17
Barnard Av. DL14: Bish A . . . 3H 3
Barnard Cl. DL5: Newt A . . . 2G 11
Barnard St. DL3: Darl . . . 1G 19
Barnes Cl. DL3: Darl . . . 6C 14
Barnes Rd. DL3: Darl . . . 6B 14
Barnes Wlk. DL5: Newt A . . . 3F 11
Barningham St. DL3: Darl . . . 6G 15
Barrett Rd. DL3: Darl . . . 2C 18
Barrington Mdws.
DL14: Bish A . . . 3F 3
Barrington Rd. DL5: Newt A . . . 5E 11
Barron St. DL3: Darl . . . 5G 15
Bartlett St. DL3: Darl . . . 5G 15
Barton Cl. DL5: Newt A . . . 3D 10
Barton St. DL1: Darl . . . 6A 16
Bassenthwaite Gro.
DL14: W Auc . . . 2B 6
Bates Av. DL3: Darl . . . 4C 14
Bates Cl. DL5: Newt A . . . 3E 11
Batt La. DL5: Heigh . . . 6A 12
Baxby Ter. DL2: Hur P . . . 5D 24
Baydale Rd. DL3: Darl . . . 3C 18
Baysdale Cl. DL14: Bish A . . . 3E 3
Baysdale Gdns. DL4: Shil . . . 2G 9
Baytree Rd. DL1: Darl . . . 1H 15
Beacon Grange Pk.
DL2: Sadb . . . 2H 17
Beacon Hill DL2: Sadb . . . 3H 17
Beaconsfield St. DL3: Darl . . . 6F 15
Beauly Dr. DL1: Darl . . . 2B 16
Beaumont Cl. DL5: Newt A . . . 2F 11
Beaumont Hill DL1: Darl . . . 1H 15
Beaumont St. DL1: Darl . . . 2G 19
DL14: Bish A . . . 3H 3
Beaumont St. W. DL1: Darl . . . 2G 19
Beaumont Way DL5: Newt A . . . 2F 13
Beckett Cl. DL14: Ether D . . . 2E 3
Beck Rd. DL1: Darl . . . 6H 15
Beckside DL3: Darl . . . 3F 19
Bedale Hunt DL5: Newt A . . . 3B 10
Bedburn Dr. DL3: Darl . . . 1A 18
DL14: Bish A . . . 4E 3
Bede Cl. DL14: Esc . . . 1D 2
Bede Cres. DL5: Newt A . . . 6F 11
Bede Rd. DL3: Darl . . . 2C 18
Bedford Pl. DL14: Bish A . . . 4A 4
Bedford St. DL1: Darl . . . 3G 19
Beech Cres. DL5: Heigh . . . 3A 12
Beechers Gro. DL5: Newt A . . . 1G 11
Beeches, The DL2: Midd G . . . 3C 22
Beechfield DL5: Newt A . . . 5D 10
Beech Lodge DL2: Midd G . . . 3G 23
Beech Ri. DL1: Haugh S . . . 3D 16
Beech Rd. DL1: Haugh S . . . 3D 16
DL14: Bish A . . . 2A 4
Beech Ter. DL14: Eld L . . . 5D 4
Beechwood Av. DL3: Darl . . . 2F 19
Beechwood Dr. DL14: Bish A . . . 4A 4
Bek Rd. DL5: Newt A . . . 4G 11
Belford Gdns.
DL1: Haugh S . . . 3B 16
Belford Way DL5: Newt A . . . 4B 10
Belgrave St. DL1: Darl . . . 3A 20
Belgrave Ter. DL2: Hur P . . . 5D 24
Bellasis Cl. DL5: Newt A . . . 4G 11
Bellburn La. DL3: Darl . . . 5E 15
Belle Vue Ter. DL2: Midd G . . . 4C 22
Bell's Pl. DL3: Darl . . . 1G 19
Bell St. DL14: Bish A . . . 3H 3
Bell Wlk. DL5: Newt A . . . 5H 11
Belsay Wlk. DL1: Haugh S . . . 3B 16
Belvedere Rd. DL1: Darl . . . 3H 19
Belvoir Gro. DL14: Bish A . . . 3G 3
Benbow Wlk. DL14: Coun . . . 1F 5
(not continuous)
Bensham Rd. DL1: Darl . . . 2H 15
Beresford St. DL4: Shil . . . 4E 9
Berkeley Gro. DL14: Bish A . . . 3G 3
Berkeley Rd. DL1: Darl . . . 4H 19
Berkshire Pl. DL14: Bish A . . . 4A 4
Bernera Ct. DL1: Haugh S . . . 2C 16
Berriedale Dr. DL1: Darl . . . 2A 16
Berrybank Crest DL3: Darl . . . 5C 14
Bertie Rd. DL5: Newt A . . . 4E 11
Berwick Rd. DL3: Darl . . . 4C 14
Bethany Ct. DL5: Newt A . . . 2G 11
Beveridge Arc. DL5: Newt A . . . 4F 11
Beveridge Way
DL5: Newt A . . . 4F 11
Bewick Cres. DL5: Newt A . . . 5F 11
Bickford Ter. DL5: Ayc . . . 3F 13
Bigland Ter. DL14: Bish A . . . 4B 4
BILDERSHAW . . . 6F 7
Binchester Cft. DL5: Sch A . . . 1B 12
Birch Av. DL4: Shil . . . 2E 9
DL14: Bish A . . . 4H 3
Birches, The DL2: Hurw . . . 4H 25
Birch Gro. DL1: Darl . . . 3A 16
Birch Rd. DL1: Darl . . . 1A 16
Birkdale Rd. DL3: Darl . . . 6C 14
Biscop Cres. DL5: Newt A . . . 4G 11
BISHOP AUCKLAND . . . 1H 3
Bishop Auckland By-Pass
DL14: Auc P, Bish A . . . 5H 3
BISHOP AUCKLAND GENERAL HOSPITAL . . . 2H 3
Bishop Auckland Station (Rail)
. . . 2H 3
Bishop Cl. DL1: Haugh S . . . 4C 16
Bishop St. DL14: Bish A . . . 1H 3
Bishopton La. DL1: Gt Bur . . . 3E 17
Bisley Ct. DL1: Darl . . . 5E 17
Blackett Rd. DL1: Darl . . . 5B 16
Blackett St. DL14: Bish A . . . 2A 4
Blackmoor Cl. DL1: Darl . . . 4C 20
Blackton Cl. DL5: Newt A . . . 4C 10
BLACKWELL . . . 4E 19
Blackwell DL3: Darl . . . 5D 18
Blackwell Cl. DL3: Darl . . . 4E 19
Blackwellgate DL1: Darl . . . 2G 19
Blackwellgate Arc.
DL1: Darl . . . 2G 19
Blackwell Gro. DL3: Darl . . . 5D 18
Blackwell La. DL3: Darl . . . 4E 19
Blackwell Rdbt. DL2: Cleas . . . 5C 18
Blackwell Scar DL3: Darl . . . 4D 18
Blagden Gro. DL14: Bish A . . . 4E 3
Blair Gro. DL14: Bish A . . . 3H 3
Blake St. DL4: Shil . . . 3E 9
Blakiston Ct. DL5: Newt A . . . 1E 11
Blanchland Grn. DL3: Darl . . . 4B 14
Bland Wlk. DL5: Newt A . . . 4H 11
Blind La. DL2: Hur P, Hurw . . . 6F 25
Bliss Cl. DL3: Darl . . . 5E 15
Bloomesley Cl.
DL5: Newt A . . . 1E 11
Bloomfield Rd. DL3: Darl . . . 6E 15
Blossom Cl. DL3: Darl . . . 5E 15
Bluebell Cl. DL3: Darl . . . 5E 15
DL5: Newt A . . . 3D 10
DL14: Ether D . . . 3E 3
Bluebell Mdw. DL5: Newt A . . . 3D 10
Bluebell Way DL5: Newt A . . . 3D 10
Blythe Av. DL14: St H . . . 6D 2
Bob Hardisty Dr.
DL14: Bish A . . . 1H 3
Bob Harrison Ct. DL1: Darl . . . 4H 15
Boddy St. DL14: Bish A . . . 6G 3
Bodmin Gro. DL3: Darl . . . 1G 15
Bollihope Gro. DL14: Bish A . . . 4E 3
Bolton Cl. DL3: Darl . . . 5C 14
Bolton Gro. DL14: Bish A . . . 3G 3
Bondgate DL3: Darl . . . 1G 19
Bonemill Bank
DL14: Auc P, Bish A . . . 4B 4
Booth Wlk. DL5: Newt A . . . 3E 11
Borough Rd. DL1: Darl . . . 2H 19
Borough Rd. Ind. Est.
DL1: Darl . . . 1H 19
Boston Cl. DL1: Haugh S . . . 3A 16
Botham Gro. DL3: Darl . . . 2G 15
Bouch St. DL4: Shil . . . 4E 9
Boundary Vw. DL3: Darl . . . 6C 14
Bourne Av. DL1: Darl . . . 1B 20
Bourne Ct. DL1: Darl . . . 1B 20
Bousfield Cres.
DL5: Newt A . . . 3F 11
Bowden Ct. DL5: Newt A . . . 5G 11
Bowen Rd. DL3: Darl . . . 4D 14
Bowes Ct. DL1: Darl . . . 6A 16
Bowes Gro. DL14: Bish A . . . 3G 3
Bowes Rd. DL5: Newt A . . . 5F 11
Bowman St. DL3: Darl . . . 3H 15
Bowser St. DL14: Bish A . . . 3H 3
Boyden Cl. DL14: St H . . . 1C 6
Boyes Hill Gro. DL3: Darl . . . 1E 19
Bracken Rd. DL3: Darl . . . 6E 15
Brack's Rd. DL14: Auc P . . . 2C 4
Bradbury Rd. DL5: Newt A . . . 1E 13
Bradford Cl. DL5: Newt A . . . 6F 11
Braemar Ct. DL1: Haugh S . . . 2D 16
Brafferton Cl. DL5: Newt A . . . 2F 11
Braithwaite St. DL4: Shil . . . 2C 8
DL14: Bish A . . . 1H 3
Bramall La. DL1: Darl . . . 6D 16
Bramham Chase
DL5: Newt A . . . 4B 10
Brancepeth Cl.
DL5: Newt A . . . 2G 11
Brancepeth Gro.
DL14: Bish A . . . 3G 3
Brankin Dr. DL1: Darl . . . 4A 20
Brankin Rd. DL1: Darl . . . 4B 20
BRANKSOME . . . 4B 14
Branksome Grn. DL3: Darl . . . 4A 14
Branksome Hall Dr.
DL3: Darl . . . 4B 14
Branksome Lodge
DL3: Darl . . . 4C 14
Branksome Ter. DL3: Darl . . . 6G 15
Brantwood Ter. DL14: Bish A . . . 6G 3
Brawton Gro. DL3: Darl . . . 5F 15
Breck Rd. DL3: Darl . . . 1E 19
Brecon Side DL1: Haugh S . . . 4D 16
Brewer St. DL14: Bish A . . . 3H 3
Brian Rd. DL1: Darl . . . 3H 15
Briar Cl. DL3: Darl . . . 5D 18
Briar Wlk. DL3: Darl . . . 5D 18
Bridge Rd. DL3: Darl . . . 5D 18
DL14: Bish A . . . 1G 3
Bridge St. DL14: Bish A . . . 1H 3
Bridge Ter. DL1: Darl . . . 2A 20
Bridle, The DL5: Newt A . . . 1F 11
Brighouse Ct. DL5: Newt A . . . 2F 13
Brighton Rd. DL1: Darl . . . 3A 20
Bright St. DL1: Darl . . . 2B 20
Brignall Moor Cres.
DL1: Darl . . . 3C 20
Brinkburn Av. DL3: Darl . . . 4E 15
Brinkburn Cl. DL14: Bish A . . . 4E 3
Brinkburn Dr. DL3: Darl . . . 5E 15
Brinkburn Pond Nature Reserve
. . . 4F 15
Brinkburn Rd. DL3: Darl . . . 5D 14
Brinsley Ct. DL14: Coun . . . 1F 5
British School Yd.
DL3: Darl . . . 2G 19
Broadmeadows DL3: Darl . . . 1C 18
Broad Wlk. DL14: Bish A . . . 1B 4
Broadway, The DL1: Darl . . . 2C 20
Broadway Sth. DL1: Darl . . . 1D 20
Brockett Cl. DL5: Newt A . . . 3E 11
Brockwell Cl. DL5: Newt A . . . 2E 11
Brockwell Ct. DL14: Coun G . . . 4E 5
Broken Banks DL14: Bish A . . . 1G 3
Brompton Wlk. DL3: Darl . . . 2D 18
Brook Cl. DL5: Newt A . . . 2G 11

A-Z Darlington 27

Farndale Gdns. DL4: Shil . . . 2F **9**
Farndale Sq. DL14: Bish A . . . 4F **3**
Farnham Cl. DL5: Newt A . . . 2G **11**
DL14: Auc P . . . 3B **4**
Farrer St. DL3: Darl . . . 5G **15**
Farrholme DL3: Darl . . . 5D **18**
Faulkner Rd. DL5: Newt A . . . 4F **11**
FAVERDALE . . . **3D 14**
Faverdale DL3: Darl . . . 3D **14**
Faverdale Black Path
DL3: Darl . . . 4E **15**
Faverdale Ind. Est.
DL3: Darl . . . 3E **15**
Faverdale Nth. DL3: Darl . . . 3E **15**
Faverdale Rd. DL3: Darl . . . 3D **14**
Faverdale W. DL3: Darl . . . 3E **15**
Faversham Pk. DL3: Darl . . . 3D **14**
Fawn Cl. DL5: Newt A . . . 1G **11**
Feetham Av. DL1: Haugh S . . . 4D **16**
Feethams DL1: Darl . . . 2G **19**
Feethams Sth. DL1: Darl . . . 2G **19**
Felton Cl. DL5: Newt A . . . 3G **11**
Fenby Av. DL1: Darl . . . 4B **20**
Fenhall Grn. DL5: Newt A . . . 2E **11**
Ferens Ter. DL4: Shil . . . 4E **9**
Fernlea Ct. DL1: Darl . . . 4A **20**
Festings Ho. *DL1: Darl . . . 6C 16*
(off Ayresome Way)
Fewston Cl. DL5: Newt A . . . 4B **10**
Fieldon Dr. DL14: W Auc . . . 1C **6**
Field St. DL1: Darl . . . 5H **15**
Fife Rd. DL3: Darl . . . 2F **19**
Fighting Cocks Junc.
DL2: Midd G . . . 2B **22**
Finchale Cres. DL3: Darl . . . 5B **14**
Finchale Rd. DL5: Newt A . . . 6F **11**
Finchale Sq. DL14: St H . . . 1D **6**
Finkle St. DL14: Bish A . . . 1H **3**
Firs, The DL1: Haugh S . . . 3C **16**
FIRTH MOOR . . . **3D 20**
Firthmoor Cres. DL1: Darl . . . 3C **20**
Firth Moor Ind. Est.
DL1: Darl . . . 3E **21**
Firtree DL4: Shil . . . 2E **9**
Fitzwilliam Dr. DL1: Darl . . . 4H **15**
Flambard Dr. DL14: Auc P . . . 2C **4**
Flamingo Cl. DL1: Darl . . . 2C **20**
Fleet St. DL14: Bish A . . . 3H **3**
Flintoff St. DL14: Bish A . . . 1A **4**
Flora Av. DL3: Darl . . . 2E **19**
Florence St. DL1: Darl . . . 2A **20**
Flynn Ct. DL5: Newt A . . . 5G **11**
Forcett St. DL3: Darl . . . 5D **14**
Ford Way DL14: Bish A . . . 5G **3**
Fore Bondgate DL14: Bish A . . . 1H **3**
Forest Moor Rd. DL1: Darl . . . 4C **20**
Forfar Ct. DL1: Haugh S . . . 2C **16**
Forge Way DL1: Darl . . . 5H **15**
Forresters Path DL5: Sch A . . . 1B **12**
Forster Cl. DL5: Newt A . . . 1D **10**
Forster M. *DL3: Darl . . . 1G 19*
(off Skinnergate)
Forster St. DL3: Darl . . . 6G **15**
Fotheringhay Dr.
DL1: Haugh S . . . 2D **16**
Foundry St. DL4: Shil . . . 1E **9**
Fountains Sq. DL14: St H . . . 1D **6**
Fountains Vw. DL3: Darl . . . 5C **14**
Four Riggs DL3: Darl . . . 1G **19**
Fowler Rd. DL5: Newt A . . . 4G **11**
Fox Cl. DL2: Hur P . . . 5E **25**
Foxglove Cl. DL5: Newt A . . . 2D **10**
Foxglove Dr. DL14: Ether D . . . 3E **3**
Fox Pl. DL5: Newt A . . . 3E **11**
Foxton Cl. DL5: Newt A . . . 3F **11**
Frances Ter. DL14: Bish A . . . 4H **3**
Fraser Ct. DL14: Coun . . . 1F **5**
Frederick St. DL14: Coun . . . 1F **5**
Freeman's Pl. DL1: Darl . . . 1H **19**
Freville Gro. DL3: Darl . . . 1B **18**
Freville St. DL4: Shil . . . 2D **8**
Friars Pardon DL2: Hurw . . . 4F **25**
Friends School Yd.
DL3: Darl . . . 2G **19**
Front, The DL2: Midd R . . . 6C **22**
Front Row DL14: Eld . . . 5E **5**
Front St. *DL14: Bish A . . . 2A 4*
(off Beech Rd.)
DL14: Ether D . . . 3E **3**
DL14: W Auc . . . 2C **6**
(not continuous)
Fryer Cres. DL1: Haugh S . . . 4D **16**
Fulbeck Rd. DL5: Newt A . . . 2F **13**
Fulford Pl. DL3: Darl . . . 3H **15**
Fulthorpe Av. DL3: Darl . . . 1B **18**
Fulthorpe Cl. DL3: Darl . . . 1C **18**
Fulthorpe Gro. DL3: Darl . . . 1B **18**
Fulton Ct. DL4: Shil . . . 1D **8**
Furguson Ct. DL14: Bish A . . . 3H **3**
Furnace Ind. Est. DL4: Shil . . . 3D **8**
Furness Cl. DL14: Bish A . . . 4E **3**
Furness St. DL1: Haugh S . . . 3B **16**

G

Gables, The DL2: Hurw . . . 4G **25**
DL14: Bish A . . . 1G **3**
Gainsborough Ct. DL1: Darl . . . 3H **19**
DL14: Bish A . . . 1H 3
(off Grainger St.)
Galloway DL1: Haugh S . . . 2D **16**
Gamul Cl. DL5: Newt A . . . 2D **10**
Garburn Pl. DL5: Newt A . . . 4D **10**
Garbutt Cl. DL4: Shil . . . 1C **8**
Garbutt Sq. DL1: Darl . . . 2A **20**
Garbutt St. DL4: Shil . . . 1C **8**
Garden Pl. DL3: Darl . . . 2H **15**
Garden St. DL1: Darl . . . 1H **19**
Garden Ter. DL14: Bish A . . . 2H **3**
Garrick Ct. *DL1: Darl . . . 2A 20*
(off King William St.)
Garsdale Ct. *DL3: Darl . . . 2G 19*
(off Larchfield St.)
Garth, The DL5: Sch A . . . 1B **12**
Garthlands DL5: Heigh . . . 6B **12**
Garthlands Rd. DL3: Darl . . . 5D **14**
Garth Mdws. DL14: H Eth . . . 6B **2**
Garthorne Av. DL3: Darl . . . 1B **18**
Gatcombe Cl.
DL5: Newt A . . . 2G **11**
Gate Ho. Cl. DL1: Haugh S . . . 3D **16**
Gateway, The DL1: Darl . . . 3A **16**
Gaunless Ter. DL14: Bish A . . . 4C **4**
General Boucher Ct.
DL14: Bish A . . . 3A **4**
Geneva Cres. DL1: Darl . . . 4A **20**
Geneva Dr. DL1: Darl . . . 4A **20**
Geneva Gdns. DL1: Darl . . . 4A **20**
Geneva La. DL1: Darl . . . 4A **20**
Geneva Rd. DL1: Darl . . . 4A **20**
Geneva Ter. DL1: Darl . . . 3H **19**
Gent Rd. DL14: Bish A . . . 3A **4**
George Reynolds Ind. Est.
DL4: Shil . . . 5F **9**
George Short Cl. DL1: Darl . . . 5H **15**
George Stephenson Dr.
DL3: Darl . . . 3D **14**
George St. DL1: Darl . . . 2H **19**
DL4: Shil . . . 2C **8**
DL14: Bish A . . . 1H **3**
(not continuous)
DL14: W Auc . . . 2B **6**
Gibbon St. DL14: Bish A . . . 1H **3**
Gib Chare DL14: Bish A . . . 1A **4**
Gibson St. DL14: Coun G . . . 5E **5**
Gilderdale Ct. DL3: Darl . . . 2D **14**
Gilling Cres. DL1: Darl . . . 3B **20**
Gilpin Ct. DL5: Newt A . . . 6G **11**
Gilpin Rd. DL5: Newt A . . . 5G **11**
Gilsland Cres.
DL1: Haugh S . . . 3B **16**
Girton Wlk. DL1: Darl . . . 4A **16**
Gladstone St. DL3: Darl . . . 1G **19**
Glaisdale Gdns. DL4: Shil . . . 2F **9**
Glamis Rd. DL1: Haugh S . . . 3C **16**
Glamis Ter. DL14: Even . . . 5A **6**
Glanton Ct. DL3: Darl . . . 2D **14**
Glebe Rd. DL1: Darl . . . 2A **16**
Glendale Dr. DL3: Darl . . . 4E **19**
Gleneagles Rd.
DL1: Haugh S . . . 2C **16**
Glenfield Rd. DL3: Darl . . . 4E **19**
Globe Cl. DL1: Darl . . . 2A **20**
Gloucester Pl. DL1: Darl . . . 5B **16**
Gonville Ct. DL1: Darl . . . 3A **16**
Goodison Way DL1: Darl . . . 6D **16**
Goodwood Cl. DL2: Sadb . . . 1H **17**
Gordon Cl. DL1: Haugh S . . . 2D **16**
Gordon La. DL14: Rams . . . 4A **6**
Gordon Ter. DL14: Bish A . . . 1H **3**
Gort Rd. DL5: Newt A . . . 4F **11**
Gouldsmith Gdns.
DL1: Haugh S . . . 4D **16**
Grace Ct. DL3: Darl . . . 1G **19**
Graham Ct. DL1: Darl . . . 2A **20**
Grainger St. DL1: Darl . . . 3H **19**
DL14: Bish A . . . 1H **3**
Grange, The DL5: Newt A . . . 1F **11**
Grange Av. DL2: Hur P . . . 4D **24**
DL14: Auc P . . . 3C **4**
Grange Ct. DL5: Newt A . . . 2G **11**
Grangemoor Cl. DL1: Darl . . . 4C **20**
Grange Rd. DL1: Darl . . . 5E **19**
Grangeside DL3: Darl . . . 4E **19**
Grange Vw. DL14: C'gate . . . 1D **4**
Grantly DL3: Darl . . . 6D **14**
Granton Cl. DL3: Darl . . . 2C **18**
Granville Av. DL4: Shil . . . 2D **8**
Granville Cl. DL4: Shil . . . 2D **8**
Granville Rd. DL14: Bish A . . . 3G **3**
Grasmere Av. DL14: W Auc . . . 2B **6**
Grasmere Rd. DL1: Darl . . . 3A **20**
Grassholme DL1: Darl . . . 3B **20**
Grassholme Pl.
DL5: Newt A . . . 4C **10**
Grass St. DL1: Darl . . . 4H **15**
Gray St. DL14: Eld L . . . 5D **4**
GREAT BURDON . . . **3E 17**
Great Gates DL14: Bish A . . . 1A **4**
Greathead Cres.
DL5: Newt A . . . 5G **11**
Great Nth. Rd. DL5: Ayc . . . 3G **13**
DL17: Rush . . . 1H **11**
Green, The DL1: Braff . . . 6H **13**
DL2: Hurw . . . 4F **25**
DL5: Ayc . . . 3G **13**
DL14: Even . . . 6B **6**
Greenbank Ct. DL3: Darl . . . 6F **15**
Greenbank Rd. DL3: Darl . . . 6F **15**
Greencroft Cl. DL3: Darl . . . 2E **19**
Greencroft Ct. DL3: Darl . . . 3F **19**
Greenfield Cl. DL2: Hurw . . . 3F **25**
Greenfields Ind. Est.
DL14: Bish A . . . 5F **3**
Greenfields Rd.
DL14: Bish A, H Eth, St H
. . . 5C **2**
Greenfield Way
DL5: Newt A . . . 4B **10**
Greenhill Rd. DL5: Heigh . . . 6A **12**
Greenhills DL3: Darl . . . 2F **19**
Green La.
DL1: Darl, Haugh S . . . 1A **16**
DL4: Shil . . . 6E **5**
DL5: Ayc . . . 3H **13**
DL14: Bish A . . . 1H **3**
(Prince's St.)
DL14: Bish A . . . 1H **7**
(W. Auckland Rd.)
DL14: Eld L . . . 5D **4**
Greenlee Gth. DL5: Newt A . . . 4C **10**
Greenmount Rd. DL3: Darl . . . 3F **19**
Greenrigg Cl. DL3: Darl . . . 2D **14**
Greensfield Cl. DL3: Darl . . . 2D **14**
Greenside Ct. DL2: Hurw . . . 4F **25**
Green St. DL1: Darl . . . 2A **20**
Greenway, The
DL2: Midd G . . . 4B **22**
Greenwell Rd. DL5: Newt A . . . 4F **11**
Grn. Wells Gth. DL14: Coun . . . 1G **5**
Greenwell St. DL1: Darl . . . 3H **19**
Gregory Ct. DL5: Newt A . . . 6F **11**
Grendon Gdns.
DL2: Midd G . . . 3B **22**
Gresham Cl. DL1: Darl . . . 4A **16**
Greville Way DL5: Newt A . . . 5F **11**
Greyfriars Cl. DL3: Darl . . . 2A **18**
Grey Gdns. DL14: Coun . . . 1F **5**
Greystones Dr. DL3: Darl . . . 6D **14**
Grey St. DL1: Darl . . . 6A **16**
DL14: Bish A . . . 2H **3**
Grindon Ct. DL5: Newt A . . . 2G **11**
Grindon Way DL5: Newt A . . . 4E **13**
Grinton Pk. Way DL1: Darl . . . 4B **20**
Groat Av. DL5: Newt A . . . 1F **13**
Groat Dr. DL5: Newt A . . . 6G **11**
Groat Rd. DL5: Newt A . . . 1G **13**
Groat Way DL5: Newt A . . . 1G **13**
Grosvenor St. DL1: Darl . . . 3H **19**
Grove Rd. DL14: Bish A . . . 2G **3**
Guardian Ct. DL3: Darl . . . 2F **19**
Gudmunsen Av. DL14: Bish A . . . 5F **3**
Guildford Cl. DL1: Haugh S . . . 4D **16**
Gunnerton Cl. DL3: Darl . . . 2D **14**
Gunn La. DL5: Newt A . . . 5H **11**
Gurlish Way DL14: Coun . . . 1F **5**
Gurney St. DL1: Darl . . . 5H **15**
Gurney Ter. DL14: Coun G . . . 4E **5**
Gurney Way DL5: Newt A . . . 1E **13**
Guthrum Pl. DL5: Newt A . . . 2E **11**
(not continuous)

H

Hackworth Cl. DL4: Shil . . . 3E **9**
DL5: Newt A . . . 6G **11**
Hackworth Ho. DL4: Shil . . . 1D **8**
Hackworth Ind. Pk. DL4: Shil . . . 4C **8**
Hackworth Rd. DL4: Shil . . . 3C **8**
Hackworth St. DL4: Shil . . . 2E **9**
Hadrian Ct. DL3: Darl . . . 3F **19**
Haggs La. DL4: Shil . . . 3H **7**
DL14: W Auc . . . 2H **7**
Haig St. DL3: Darl . . . 4G **15**
Hallimond Rd. DL14: Esc . . . 2D **2**
Hallington Head
DL5: Newt A . . . 4B **10**
Hall La. DL5: Heigh . . . 5B **12**
Hall Vw. Gro. DL3: Darl . . . 6B **14**
Halnaby Av. DL3: Darl . . . 1A **18**
Hambleton Ct. DL5: Newt A . . . 3C **10**
Hambleton Gro.
DL1: Haugh S . . . 3B **16**
Hambleton Rd. DL14: Coun . . . 1G **5**
Hamilton Dr. DL1: Darl . . . 2B **16**
Hammond Dr. DL1: Darl . . . 4G **19**
Hampshire Pl. DL14: Bish A . . . 4A **4**
Hamsterley Rd.
DL5: Newt A . . . 3D **10**
Hamsterley St. DL3: Darl . . . 5F **15**
Hanover Cl. DL3: Darl . . . 2B **18**
Hanover Ct. DL14: Bish A . . . 3A **4**
Hanover Gdns.
DL14: Bish A . . . 3A **4**
Hansard Cl. DL5: Sch A . . . 1B **12**
Hansons Bldgs.
DL2: Midd G . . . 4C **22**
Harcourt St. DL3: Darl . . . 5G **15**
Hardes La. DL5: Redw . . . 2A **12**
Hardinge Rd. DL5: Newt A . . . 4F **11**
Harding Ter. DL3: Darl . . . 5F **15**
Hardisty Cres. DL14: Bish A . . . 4G **3**
Hardwick Cl. DL1: Haugh S . . . 3C **16**
Hardwick Ct. DL5: Newt A . . . 3F **11**
Harebell Mdws.
DL5: Newt A . . . 1F **11**
Hareson Rd. DL5: Newt A . . . 3C **10**
Harewood Gro. DL3: Darl . . . 3F **19**
Harewood Hill DL3: Darl . . . 3F **19**
Harewood Ter. DL3: Darl . . . 3F **19**
Hargreave Ter. DL1: Darl . . . 2H **19**
Harker St. DL4: Shil . . . 2D **8**
Harland Ct. DL14: St H . . . 1D **6**
Harley Gro. DL1: Haugh S . . . 3D **16**
Harpers Ter. DL2: Midd G . . . 2B **22**
Harringay Cres. DL1: Darl . . . 6D **16**
Harrison Cl. DL4: Shil . . . 4E **9**
Harrison Cres. DL14: Bish A . . . 5F **3**
Harrison Ter. DL3: Darl . . . 5F **15**
Harris St. DL1: Darl . . . 3B **20**
HARROWGATE HILL . . . **2A 16**
HARROWGATE VILLAGE . . . **1H 15**
Harry St. DL3: Darl . . . 4G **15**
Hartford Rd. DL3: Darl . . . 3E **19**
Harthope Gro. DL14: Bish A . . . 4F **3**
Hartington Way DL3: Darl . . . 4F **15**
Hartley Av. DL14: Leeh . . . 1G **5**
Hartley Rd. DL5: Newt A . . . 4F **11**
Harts Bldgs. DL2: Midd G . . . 3C **22**
Haselrigg Cl. DL5: Sch A . . . 1B **12**
Haslewood Rd.
DL5: Newt A . . . 1E **11**
Hatfield Rd. DL5: Newt A . . . 5G **11**
Hatfield Way DL14: Bish A . . . 5B **4**
Haughton Grn.
DL1: Haugh S . . . 5C **16**
HAUGHTON LE SKERNE . . . **4D 16**
Haughton Rd.
DL1: Darl, Haugh S . . . 1H **19**
Havelock Cl. DL5: Newt A . . . 5G **11**
Havelock St. DL1: Darl . . . 5H **15**
Haven Cl. DL1: Darl . . . 1B **20**
Haven Gdns. DL1: Darl . . . 1B **20**
Hawes Pl. DL5: Newt A . . . 4D **10**
Haweswater Gro.
DL14: W Auc . . . 2B **6**
Hawkesbury M. DL3: Darl . . . 6F **15**
Hawkhead Pl. DL5: Newt A . . . 4D **10**
Hawkshead Ct.
DL5: Newt A . . . 4D **10**

Lawrence St. DL1: Darl 2A 20
Layton Ct. DL5: Newt A 2F 11
Lazenby Cl. DL3: Darl 6C 14
Lazenby Cres. DL3: Darl 6C 14
Lazenby Gro. DL3: Darl 6C 14
Leach Gro. DL3: Darl 4D 14
Leadenhall St. DL1: Darl 6H 15
Leafield Rd. DL1: Darl 3H 19
Leas, The DL1: Darl 2H 15
Leaside DL5: Newt A 1F 13
Leaside Nth. DL5: Newt A 1F 13
Leazes Cl. DL14: St H 1C 6
Leazes La. DL14: St H 5C 2
Leconfield Cl. DL3: Darl 2F 19
Lee Grn. DL5: Newt A 6F 11
LEEHOLME 1H 5
Leeholme Rd. DL14: Leeh 1G 5
Leicester Gro.
   DL1: Haugh S 4D 16
Leith Rd. DL3: Darl 1B 18
Leonard St. DL1: Darl 3A 20
Leopold Pl. DL14: Bish A 2A 4
Leslie St. DL14: St H 1D 6
Leven Gdns. DL1: Darl 2B 16
Leven Rd. DL14: W Auc 2B 6
Lewes Rd. DL1: Darl 3A 20
Lewis Cl. DL2: Croft T 5C 24
Leyburn Rd. DL1: Darl 4H 15
Liddell Cl. DL5: Newt A 4H 11
Lightfoot Rd. DL5: Newt A 4E 11
Lilac Cl. DL4: Shil 3F 9
Lilac Way DL14: Toft H 6A 2
Lilburn Cl. DL4: Shil 1D 8
Lilburne Cres. DL5: Newt A 4F 11
Lime Av. DL1: Darl 1H 15
Lime Gro. DL4: Shil 2F 9
   DL14: Bish A 5H 3
Limehurst Rd. DL3: Darl 6F 15
Lime La. DL1: Braff 5G 13
Lime Ter. DL14: Eld L 5D 4
Linacre Way DL1: Darl 3A 16
Linburn Dr. DL14: Bish A 4E 3
Lincoln Cl. DL5: Newt A 4H 11
Lincoln Cl. DL1: Haugh S 4D 16
Lincoln St. DL14: Leeh 1H 5
Linden Av. DL3: Darl 2E 19
Linden Cl. DL4: Shil 3F 9
Linden Ct. DL2: Hur P 5D 24
Linden Dr. DL2: Hur P 5D 24
   DL3: Darl 3E 19
Linden Pl. DL5: Newt A 5C 10
Linden Rd. DL14: Bish A 3A 4
Lindisfarne Cl.
   DL14: Ether D 3E 3
Lindisfarne Ct.
   DL1: Haugh S 4C 16
Lindsay St. DL14: Bish A 2G 3
Lingard Wlk. DL5: Newt A 6G 11
LINGFIELD 1D 20
Lingfield Cl. DL1: Darl 1D 20
Lingfield Est. DL1: Darl 6D 16
Lingfield Grn. DL1: Darl 1D 20
Lingfield Way DL1: Darl 3E 21
Lingford Ct. DL14: Bish A 2H 3
Lingmell Dene DL14: Coun 1F 5
Linwood Gro. DL3: Darl 4E 19
Lisle Rd. DL5: Newt A 3C 10
Lismore Dr. DL1: Haugh S 2C 16
Littlebeck Dr. DL1: Haugh S 4B 16
Little La. DL5: Ayc 3G 13
Lock St. DL3: Darl 4G 15
Lockyer Cl. DL5: Newt A 3D 10
Locomotion 4F 9
Locomotion La. DL3: Darl 4D 14
Locomotive St.
   DL1: Haugh S 3B 16
Lodge St. DL1: Darl 1H 19
Lombard Cl. DL1: Darl 3F 19
   (off Marlborough Dr.)
Lomond Wlk. DL14: W Auc 2C 6
Longfield Rd. DL3: Darl 3G 15
   DL14: Bish A 5A 4
Long Tens Way
   DL5: Newt A 5E 13
   (not continuous)
Loraine Cres. DL1: Darl 4G 19
Loraine Wlk. DL5: Newt A 3E 11
Lorne Ter. DL14: Coun 1G 5
Lorn Wlk. DL1: Haugh S 2C 16
Louisa St. DL1: Darl 2A 20
Louisa Ter. DL14: St H 6E 3
Low Deanery St. DL14: Eld L 5D 4

Lowery Rd. DL5: Newt A 5E 11
Lowe St. DL3: Darl 1G 19
Loweswater Gro.
   DL14: W Auc 2B 6
LOW ETHERLEY 5B 2
Lowfields DL5: Sch A 1B 12
Low Grn. DL5: Newt A 1G 11
Low Melbourne St.
   DL14: Bish A 4H 3
Lowmoor Rd. DL1: Darl 4C 20
Lowson St. DL3: Darl 3H 15
Lowther Dr. DL1: Darl 4A 20
   DL5: Newt A 2G 11
Lowther Rd. DL14: Bish A 5G 3
Lucknow St. DL1: Darl 6A 16
Lumley Cl. DL5: Newt A 5F 11
Lumley Gro. DL14: Bish A 3G 3
Lunedale Rd. DL1: Darl 6C 14
Lupin Cl. DL14: Ether D 2E 3
Lusby Cres. DL14: Bish A 5F 3
Lutterington Grn. La.
   DL14: Even G, W Auc 6C 6
Lutterington La.
   DL14: W Auc 5D 6
Luttryngton Ct. DL5: Newt A 3C 10
Lych Ga. DL2: Hurw 4G 25
Lynne Cl. DL3: Darl 2H 15
Lynton Gdns. DL1: Darl 2C 20
Lyonette Rd. DL1: Haugh S 3B 16
Lyon Wlk. DL5: Newt A 5F 11
Lytham St. DL1: Darl 2A 16

M

Maben Av. DL14: St H 6D 2
McCullagh Gdns.
   DL14: Bish A 3A 4
McIntyre Ter. DL14: Bish A 3H 3
Mackenzie Pl. DL5: Newt A 3E 11
Macmillan Rd. DL5: Newt A 4E 11
McMullen Rd. DL1: Darl 5C 16
McNay St. DL3: Darl 5G 15
Maddison St. DL4: Shil 3D 8
Mafeking Pl. DL4: Shil 2E 9
Magnet St. DL4: Shil 3E 9
Magnolia Cl. DL5: Sch A 2C 12
Magnolia Way DL4: Shil 2F 9
Main Rd. DL14: Eld 5E 5
Main St. DL4: Shil 2D 8
   DL14: Bish A 4B 4
   DL14: Wit P 1A 2
Major St. DL3: Darl 5F 15
Malham Cres. DL5: Newt A 3D 10
Malim Rd. DL1: Darl 2D 20
Maling Grn. DL5: Newt A 4G 11
Mallard Rd. DL1: Darl 2D 20
Mallards, The DL4: Shil 4D 8
Mallory Ct. DL1: Darl 5D 16
Maltby Cl. DL1: Auc P 3C 4
Maltkiln La. DL5: Ayc 3G 13
Malvern Cl. DL2: Hurw 4G 25
Malvern Cres. DL3: Darl 4A 14
Malvern Wlk. DL14: Coun 1G 5
Malvern Way DL5: Newt A 4B 10
Manor Cl. DL5: Heigh 4A 12
   DL14: Even 6B 6
Manorfields DL2: Hurw 4G 25
Manor Rd. DL2: Hur P 4D 24
   DL3: Darl 3F 19
   DL14: St H 1D 6
Manor St. DL14: Even 6B 6
Mansley Ct. DL3: Darl 5F 15
Manston Ct. DL2: Midd G 3C 22
Maple Av. DL4: Shil 2F 9
Maple Cl. DL14: Toft H 6A 2
Maple Lodge DL2: Midd G 3G 23
Maple Rd. DL1: Darl 1A 16
Marazion Dr. DL1: Darl 1G 15
Marburn Pl. DL3: Darl 6G 15
Margaret Ter. DL14: Bish A 5C 4
Marigold Ct. DL1: Darl 1B 20
Marina Rd. DL3: Darl 1H 15
Market Pl. DL1: Darl 2G 19
   DL4: Shil 1E 9
   DL14: Bish A 1A 4
Markham Pl. DL5: Newt A 4H 11
Marlborough Dr. DL1: Darl 3F 19
Marley Rd. DL5: Newt A 4H 11
Marrick Av. DL1: Darl 2A 14
Marrick Cl. DL5: Newt A 4D 10
Marsden Wlk. DL3: Darl 2H 15
Marshall Rd. DL5: Newt A 4E 11

Marshall St. DL3: Darl 6G 15
Marske Gro. DL3: Darl 4G 15
Marston Moor Rd.
   DL1: Darl 3D 20
Martindale Rd.
   DL1: Haugh S 4A 16
Marwood Cres. DL3: Darl 4E 15
Mary Ct. DL3: Darl 5C 14
Mary Ter. DL14: Bish A 5C 4
Masham Moor Way
   DL1: Darl 4C 20
Matthew Cl. DL5: Newt A 3H 11
Maude St. DL3: Darl 1G 19
Maude Ter.
   DL14: Bish A, St H 1D 6
Maud Ter. DL14: Even 4A 6
Maughan St. DL4: Shil 2D 8
Maxwell Cl. DL3: Darl 3C 20
Mayfair Rd. DL1: Darl 2H 15
Mayfield Cl. DL3: Darl 2F 19
Mayfield Wlk. DL14: St H 1D 6
Mayflower Cl. DL1: Darl 2B 20
May St. DL14: Bish A 1H 3
Mead, The DL1: Darl 2B 20
Meadowfield Rd. DL3: Darl 4C 14
Meadowfield Way
   DL5: Newt A 3C 10
Meadow Ri. DL5: Newt A 1C 18
Meadows, The
   DL2: Midd G 4C 22
   DL5: Middr 2A 10
Meadows Edge DL5: Middr ..2A 10
Meadow Vw. DL14: W Auc 1C 6
Meatlesburn Cl. DL5: Sch A 1B 12
Mechanics' Yd. DL3: Darl 2G 19
Meet, The DL5: Newt A 3B 10
Mellanby Cres.
   DL5: Newt A 4H 11
Melland Ct. DL1: Darl 2H 19
Melland St. DL1: Darl 2H 19
Mellor Ct. DL1: Darl 2H 19
Melrose Av. DL3: Darl 2H 15
Melrose Dr. DL14: St H 1C 6
Melsonby Cres. DL1: Darl 3B 20
Melville St. DL3: Darl 6G 15
Mendip Gro.
   DL1: Haugh S 4B 16
Mendip Wlk. DL14: Coun 1G 5
Menom Rd. DL5: Newt A 3F 13
Menville Cl. DL5: Newt A 6B 10
Mercia Ct. DL3: Darl 1G 19
Merton Cl. DL1: Darl 3A 16
Merz Rd. DL5: Newt A 5F 11
Mewburn Ct. DL3: Darl 2G 15
Mewburn Rd. DL3: Darl 2G 15
Meynell Rd. DL3: Darl 4G 15
Mickle Gro. DL14: Leeh 1G 5
Middleham Rd. DL1: Darl 2A 16
Middleham Way
   DL5: Newt A 2G 11
Middlehope Gro.
   DL14: Bish A 4E 3
Middleton La. DL2: Midd G 4C 22
MIDDLETON ONE ROW 6D 22
Middleton Rd. DL2: Sadb 2H 17
   DL4: Shil 3D 8
MIDDLETON ST GEORGE ...3B 22
Middlewood Av. DL14: St H 1D 6
MIDDRIDGE 2A 10
Middridge Drift Ind. Est.
   DL4: Shil 1G 9
Middridge Farms
   DL5: Middr 4A 10
Middridge La. DL4: Shil 1E 9
Middridge Rd. DL5: Middr ..1E 9
Middridge Rd. DL5: Newt A ..2B 10
   (not continuous)
Midfields DL5: Sch A 1B 12
Milbank Ct. DL3: Darl 1D 18
Milbank Cres. DL3: Darl 1E 18
Milbank Rd. DL3: Darl 1D 18
Mildred St. DL3: Darl 6G 15
Milford Mdw. DL14: Bish A 5B 4
Milkwood Ct. DL3: Darl 1A 20
Millbank DL5: Heigh 6B 12
Millbank Cl. DL14: W Auc 2C 6
Millbank Ter. DL14: Eld L 5D 4
Millennium Way
   DL5: Newt A 5E 13
Millfields DL5: Ayc 2H 13

Mill La. DL1: Haugh S 5D 16
   DL2: Midd G 3D 22
   (not continuous)
   DL5: Redw 6G 9
   DL14: Bish A 4B 4
Mill Race, The DL2: Croft T 5C 24
Millrace Cl. DL1: Haugh S 3D 16
Mills Cl. DL5: Newt A 5E 11
Mill St. DL4: Shil 3E 9
Milner Rd. DL1: Darl 3H 19
Milton Av. DL14: Bish A 3H 3
Milton St. DL1: Darl 2B 20
Minors Cres. DL3: Darl 4B 14
Minster Wlk. DL2: Hurw 4G 25
Mistral Dr. DL1: Darl 2A 16
Model Pl. DL1: Darl 2A 16
Moffat St. DL1: Haugh S 2C 16
Monarch Grn. DL1: Darl 2A 16
Monk End DL2: Croft T 5C 24
Monkend Ter. DL2: Croft T 5C 24
Monks End DL5: Ayc 3H 13
Montagu Ct. DL1: Darl 3F 19
   (off Marlborough Dr.)
Monteith Cl. DL14: W Auc 2C 6
Montrose St. DL1: Darl 6H 15
Moore La. DL5: Newt A 5H 11
Moore St. DL14: Eld L 5D 4
Moorfield Cl. DL1: Darl 4C 20
Moorlands Rd. DL3: Darl 5D 14
Moor La. DL4: Old E 6H 5
   DL5: Newt A 1B 10
Moray Cl. DL1: Haugh S 2D 16
Morland St. DL14: Bish A 4H 3
Mornington La. DL3: Darl 5E 15
Morpeth Av. DL1: Haugh S 4B 16
Morpeth Dr. DL14: Bish A 3G 3
Morrison Cl. DL5: Newt A 2F 11
Morton Cl. DL14: Auc P 3D 4
MORTON PALMS 3G 21
Morton Pk. DL1: Darl 3F 21
Morton Retail Pk. DL1: Darl ..3F 21
Morton Rd. DL1: Darl 3F 21
Morton Wlk. DL5: Newt A 4G 11
Mossbank Gro.
   DL1: Haugh S 4B 16
Moule Cl. DL5: Newt A 6E 11
Moulton Way DL1: Darl 3B 20
Mt. Pleasant Cl.
   DL2: Midd G 3C 22
Mowbray Dr. DL2: Hurw 3F 25
MOWDEN 6B 14
Mowden Hall Dr. DL3: Darl 6C 14
Mowden St. DL3: Darl 6G 15
Mowden Ter. DL3: Darl 6G 15
Mowden Wlk. DL3: Darl 6B 14
Muirkirk Gro. DL1: Haugh S ..3B 16
Mulgrave Ct. DL5: Newt A 2G 11
Mulheim Cl. DL3: Darl 4D 14
Murphy Cres. DL14: Bish A 4G 3
Murray Av. DL14: Bish A 4G 3
Murrayfield Way DL1: Darl 6D 16
Murray Wlk. DL3: Darl 1C 18
Murton Cl. DL5: Ayc 3G 13
Musgrave St. DL14: St H 6E 3
Myrtle Gdns. DL1: Darl 1A 16

N

Nairn Cl. DL1: Haugh S 2D 16
Napier St. DL3: Darl 1F 19
Neasham Dr. DL1: Darl 4B 20
Neasham Rd.
   DL1: Darl, Hur M 2A 20
   DL2: Hur M, Neas 5B 20
   DL2: Hurw 4H 25
   DL2: Midd G 6H 21
Nebraska Cl. DL1: Haugh S ..3A 16
Nelson St. DL14: Bish A 1H 3
Nelson Ter. DL3: Darl 3H 19
Nestfield Ind. Est.
   DL1: Darl 5A 16
Nestfield St. DL1: Darl 5A 16
   (not continuous)
Netherby Ri. DL3: Darl 2D 18
Nevada Gdns.
   DL1: Haugh S 3A 16
Neville Cl. DL14: Even 6B 6
Neville Ho. DL1: Haugh S 3C 16
Neville Pde. DL5: Newt A 5G 11
Neville Rd. DL3: Darl 1E 19
Newark Av. DL14: Ether D 3E 3
Newbiggin La. DL2: Heigh 6C 8

New Brook Ter. DL14: Eld L 4D 4
Newburn Ct. DL5: Newt A 4E 11
New Cl. DL5: Ayc 4H 11
NEW COUNDON 1D 4
Newfoundland St. DL3: Darl ..5F 15
Newgate Cen. DL14: Bish A ...1H 3
Newgate St. DL14: Bish A 2H 3
Newholme Cres.
  DL14: Even 5A 6
Newlands Av. DL4: Shil 3E 9
  DL14: Bish A 3H 3
Newlands Rd. DL3: Darl 5E 15
New La. DL5: Newt A 2A 12
Newlyn Dr. DL3: Darl 1G 15
Newport Ct. DL1: Haugh S ...5D 16
New Row DL2: Midd G 3C 22
  DL14: Eld 5E 5
NEW SHILDON 4E 9
New St. DL14: W Auc 2C 6
NEWTON AYCLIFFE 4G 11
Newton Aycliffe Leisure Cen.
  ....5F 11
Newton Aycliffe Station (Rail)
  ....6D 10
Newton Cap Bank
  DL14: Bish A, Tor 1H 3
Newton La. DL2: Darl 1A 14
  DL3: Darl 3A 14
Nickstream La. DL3: Darl ..4C 14
Nightingale Av.
  DL1: Haugh S 3C 16
Ninefields DL14: Bish A 1H 3
Norfolk Pl. DL14: Bish A 4A 4
Northallerton Rd.
  DL2: Croft T, Dalt T 5C 24
Nth. Bondgate DL14: Bish A ..1H 3
Northcliffe DL14: Bish A 5B 4
Northcote Ter. DL3: Darl ...5F 15
North Cotts. DL5: Sch A 1C 12
Nth. Eastern Ter. DL1: Darl ..2H 19
North End Gdns.
  DL14: Bish A 3A 4
Northfield Way DL5: Newt A ..6E 11
Northgate DL1: Darl 1G 19
Northgate Ho. DL3: Darl ...1G 19
Nth. Lodge Ter. DL3: Darl ...6G 15
North Ri. DL3: Darl 3H 15
North Rd. DL1: Darl 1H 15
North Rd. Ind. Est.
  DL3: Darl 4G 15
North Road Station (Rail) ...5G 15
North Side DL5: Middr 2A 10
North Side Ct. DL5: Middr ...2A 10
Northside Ct. DL5: Middr 2A 10
North Ter. DL4: Shil 1E 9
  DL5: Ayc 3G 13
Northumberland Av.
  DL14: Bish A 3G 3
Northumberland St.
  DL3: Darl 2G 19
Norton Bk. La. DL2: Sadb ...1H 17
Norton Cres. DL2: Sadb 1H 17
Norton Rd. DL2: Sadb 1H 17
Norwich Gro. DL1: Haugh S ..4D 16
Nottingham St. DL14: Leeh ...1G 5
Nuffield Cl. DL1: Darl 3A 16
Nunnery Cl. DL3: Darl 1C 6
Nunnery La. DL3: Darl 2A 18
  (not continuous)
Nuns Cl. DL14: Bish A 4B 4
Nursery, The DL14: W Auc ...2C 6
  (off Station Rd.)

O

Oakdene Av. DL14: Darl 2F 19
Oakfield DL5: Newt A 5D 10
Oak Gro. DL1: Darl 2A 16
Oakhurst Rd. DL3: Darl 6F 15
Oakland Gdns. DL1: Darl 2H 15
Oaklands, The DL2: Midd R ..6D 22
Oaklands Ter. DL3: Darl 6G 15
Oak Lea DL1: Darl 2F 9
Oaklea Ct. DL1: Darl 2G 19
Oaklea M. DL5: Ayc 4G 13
Oaklea Ter. DL14: Bish A 3H 3
Oakley Grange
  DL14: W Auc 2C 6
Oakley Grn. DL14: W Auc 2C 6
Oak Lodge DL2: Midd G 3G 23
Oakmoor Ct. DL1: Darl 4C 20

Oaks, The DL2: Midd G 4F 23
  DL3: Darl 6E 15
  DL5: Newt A 1G 11
Oaks Bank DL14: Even 4A 6
Oak St. DL14: Eld L 5D 4
Oak Ter. DL14: Bish A 2A 4
OAK TREE 3F 23
Oaktree Cl. DL2: Midd G 4F 23
Oakwood Dr. DL1: Darl 2A 16
Oban Ct. DL1: Haugh S 3C 16
Odeon Cinema
  Darlington 6H 15
Office Row DL14: Eld 5F 5
OLD ELDON 6H 5
Old Engine Ho's. DL4: Shil ..4A 8
Old Favourite's Wlk.
  DL3: Darl 3C 14
Old Hall Farm Rd.
  DL14: St H 1D 6
Olympic St. DL3: Darl 5E 15
Oransay Wlk.
  DL1: Haugh S 2C 16
Orchard, The DL2: Sadb 2H 17
  DL5: Heigh 6B 12
Orchard Ct. DL3: Darl 6F 15
Orchard La. DL5: Ayc 3H 11
Orchard Rd. DL3: Darl 6E 15
Orchard Way DL4: Shil 1E 9
Oriel Ct. DL1: Darl 3A 16
Orkney Wlk. DL1: Haugh S ...2C 16
Orlands, The DL5: Ayc 3G 13
Osbert Pl. DL5: Newt A 3E 11
Osborne Ct. DL3: Darl 1D 18
Osborne St. DL4: Shil 2D 8
Osbourne Ter. DL14: Even ...5A 6
  DL14: Leeh 1H 5
  (off Leeholme Rd.)
Osric Pl. DL5: Newt A 3F 11
Oswald St. DL14: St H 1D 6
Otley Ter. DL3: Darl 5G 15
Otterburn Cl. DL1: Haugh S ..3B 16
Outram Ct. DL3: Darl 1F 19
  (off Outram St.)
Outram St. DL3: Darl 1F 19
Oval, The DL2: Hurw 4H 25
  DL4: Shil 1D 8
  DL14: St H 6E 3
Oxclose La. DL3: Darl 4B 14
Oxford St. DL1: Darl 6H 15
  DL4: Shil 3D 8
  DL14: Eld L 5D 4
Oxford Ter. DL14: Bish A 1H 3
OXNEYFIELD 3B 24

P

Paddock, The DL2: Midd G ...5C 22
  DL5: Newt A 1G 11
Palmer Rd. DL5: Newt A 6G 11
Palm Tree Vs.
  DL2: Midd G 3B 22
Paradise Way DL3: Darl 4D 14
Park Av. DL14: C'gate 1D 4
Park Cres. DL3: Darl 3H 19
Parkgate DL1: Darl 2H 19
Parkgate Chambers
  DL1: Darl 2H 19
Parkland Dr. DL3: Darl 6B 14
Parkland Gro. DL3: Darl 6B 14
Park La. DL1: Darl 3H 19
Park Pl. DL1: Darl 2H 19
Park Rd. DL14: Wit P 1A 2
Parkside St. DL1: Darl 4F 19
  DL14: Bish A 1A 4
Park St. DL1: Darl 2H 19
Park Vw. DL4: Shil 2D 8
Pasture Rows DL14: Eld 5F 5
Pateley Cl. DL5: Newt A 4D 10
Pateley Moor Cres.
  DL1: Darl 4B 20
Patenson Ct. DL5: Newt A ...1D 10
Pattison St. DL1: Darl 2A 20
Paulinus Rd. DL5: Newt A ...5E 11
Paxton Cl. DL5: Newt A 3D 10
Peabody St. DL3: Darl 3H 15
Pearl St. DL4: Shil 2D 8
Pears' Ter. DL4: Shil 3E 9
Pease Cotts. DL14: Darl 2G 19
Peases Row DL14: Bish A 6F 3
Pease Way DL5: Newt A 6D 10
Peebles Cl. DL1: Haugh S ...2D 16

Peel St. DL1: Darl 2A 20
  (not continuous)
  DL14: Bish A 2A 4
Pemberton Rd. DL5: Newt A ..1F 11
Pemberton Ter.
  DL2: Midd G 3C 22
Pembroke Ct. DL1: Darl 2A 20
Pembroke St. DL14: Leeh 1H 5
Pendeen Gro. DL1: Darl 1G 15
Pendleton Rd. DL1: Darl 4H 15
  (not continuous)
Pendleton Rd. Sth.
  DL1: Darl 4H 15
Pendower St. DL3: Darl 6G 15
Penney Yd. DL1: Darl 1G 19
Pennine Cl. DL3: Darl 6D 14
Pennine Wlk. DL5: Newt A ...4D 10
Penny La. DL3: Darl 3F 19
Penryn Cl. DL3: Darl 1G 15
Pensbury St. DL1: Darl 2H 19
Pentland Gro. DL3: Darl 2C 18
Percy Rd. DL3: Darl 3G 15
Percy St. DL14: Bish A 4H 3
Perth Gro. DL1: Haugh S 2D 16
Peterhouse Cl. DL1: Darl 4A 16
Peverell St. DL14: Bish A 4B 4
Philpotts Wlk. DL5: Newt A ..3G 11
Phoenix Cl. DL1: Darl 2C 20
Phoenix Pl. DL4: Shil 1E 9
  DL5: Newt A 2E 11
Pickwick Ind. Est.
  DL14: St H 1C 6
PIERREMONT 1E 19
Pierremont Cres. DL3: Darl ..1E 19
Pierremont Dr. DL3: Darl 6E 15
Pierremont Gdns. DL3: Darl ..1E 19
Pierremont Rd. DL3: Darl 5E 15
Pilkington Way DL14: Auc P ..3C 4
Pilmoor Grn. DL1: Darl 4B 20
Pine Gro. DL3: Darl 3D 18
Pine Lodge DL2: Midd G 3G 23
Pine Tree Cres. DL4: Shil 2F 9
Pinetree Gro. DL2: Midd G ..4C 22
Pinewood Cl. DL1: Darl 4C 20
  DL5: Newt A 2D 10
Pinewood Cres. DL5: Heigh ..6A 12
Pleasant Vw. DL2: Sadb 1H 17
  (off Chapel Row)
  DL3: Darl 1G 19
Polam La. DL1: Darl 2G 19
Polam Rd. DL1: Darl 3G 19
Pollard's Dr. DL14: Bish A ...2G 3
Polperro Gro. DL1: Darl 1H 15
Pondfield Cl. DL3: Darl 3C 18
Pond Vw. DL1: Darl 1B 20
Poplar Gro. DL1: Darl 1B 20
Poplar Lodge DL2: Midd G ..3G 23
Porter Cl. DL5: Newt A 3G 11
Portland Pl. DL3: Darl 1G 19
Portreath Cl. DL3: Darl 1H 15
Portrush Cl. DL1: Haugh S ..3D 16
Portsmouth Pl.
  DL1: Haugh S 5D 16
Post Horn, The
  DL5: Newt A 3B 10
Post Ho. Wynd DL3: Darl ...1G 19
Potts Rd. DL14: Leeh 1G 5
Pounteys Cl. DL2: Midd G ..4B 22
Powlett St. DL3: Darl 2G 19
Prebend Row DL1: Darl 1G 19
Prescott St. DL1: Darl 6A 16
Prescott Way DL14: Bish A ..3H 3
Preston Rd. DL5: Newt A 1E 13
Prestwick Cl. DL2: Midd G ..3C 22
Price Av. DL14: Bish A 5G 3
Priestgate DL1: Darl 1G 19
Priestman Rd. DL5: Newt A ..4E 11
Primitive St. DL4: Shil 1D 8
Primrose La. DL14: Ether D ..2E 3
Primrose St. DL3: Darl 2G 19
Princess Rd. DL1: Darl 1H 15
Princess St. DL1: Darl 2A 20
Princes St. DL4: Shil 2C 8
  DL14: Bish A 1H 3
Prior Dene DL3: Darl 5D 14
Prior St. DL3: Darl 5D 14
Priory Gro. DL14: Bish A 4C 4
Progress Way DL1: Darl 6H 15
Prospect Pl. DL1: Darl 1G 19
  (off Bondgate)
  DL3: Darl 4G 15
Proudfoot Dr. DL14: Bish A ..5G 3
Provident Ter. DL14: Even ...4A 6

Pudsey Wlk. DL1: Darl 4H 19
  DL5: Newt A 6G 11
Punch Bowl Yd. DL3: Darl ...1G 19
  (off Duke St.)

Q

Quaker La. DL1: Darl 3G 19
Quantock Cl. DL1: Haugh S ..4B 16
Quarry St. DL4: Shil 2D 8
Quebec St. DL1: Darl 1H 19
Queen's Rd. DL14: Bish A ...2A 4
Queen St. DL4: Shil 1E 9
Queen St. Cen. DL3: Darl ...1G 19
Queensway DL4: Shil 2F 9

R

Raby Dr. DL5: Newt A 1G 11
Raby Gdns. DL4: Shil 1D 8
  DL14: Bish A 3H 3
Raby St. DL3: Darl 2F 19
  DL14: Even 6B 6
Raby Ter. DL3: Darl 2G 19
  DL14: W Auc 2B 6
Raddive Cl. DL5: Newt A 2D 10
Railway Cotts. DL2: Hur M ...5A 20
Railway Ho's. DL14: Eld L ...5D 4
Railway St. DL14: Bish A 2A 4
Railway Ter. DL2: Hur P 5D 24
  DL4: Shil 3E 9
Railway Vw. DL1: Darl 4A 20
Raine St. DL14: Bish A 1H 3
Raine Wlk. DL5: Newt A 5G 11
Rainhill Way DL3: Darl 4D 14
Ramsey Cres. DL14: Bish A ..5F 3
Ramsey Pl. DL5: Newt A 4G 11
Ramsey Wlk. DL1: Haugh S ..4C 16
Ramsgill Ho. DL1: Darl 4B 20
Ramsgill Ho. DL1: Darl 4B 20
Randolph Ind. Est.
  DL14: Even 6B 6
Randolph St. DL14: Coun G ..5D 4
Randolph Ter. DL14: Even ...6B 6
Ranulf Ct. DL5: Newt A 3C 10
Ravensdale Cl. DL1: Darl 4E 19
Ravensdale Wlk. DL3: Darl ..3E 19
Ravensworth Av.
  DL14: Bish A 3H 3
Raydaleside DL3: Darl 2F 19
Rear W. La. DL14: Bish A 4F 3
Rectory La. DL2: Croft T 5C 24
Red Barnes Way DL1: Darl ...6C 16
Red Barns Bungs.
  DL1: Darl 5C 16
Red Hall Dr. DL1: Darl 6C 16
Red Ho. La. DL5: Redw 6E 9
Red Ho's. DL14: H Eth 6A 2
Redmire Cl. DL1: Darl 4H 15
Red Rose Cl. DL3: Darl 3C 14
Redruth Dr. DL3: Darl 1G 15
Redwood Cl. DL1: Darl 4D 20
Redworth Gro.
  DL14: Auc P 2C 4
Redworth Rd. DL3: Darl 5C 14
  DL4: Shil 3E 9
  DL5: Heigh 5B 12
Redworth Way DL5: Newt A ..1E 13
Reethmoor Cl. DL1: Darl 3D 20
Reeth Pl. DL5: Newt A 3D 10
Regal Dr. DL1: Darl 2A 16
Regents Cl. DL1: Darl 2B 20
Regent St. DL4: Shil 2D 8
  DL14: Bish A 1A 4
  DL14: Eld L 5D 4
Reid St. DL3: Darl 6F 15
Rembrandt Way
  DL5: Newt A 2F 13
Rennie Ct. DL1: Darl 1A 20
Rennie Wlk. DL1: Darl 1A 20
Retail Pk. DL1: Darl 6B 16
Ribble Ct. DL1: Darl 5G 19
Ribble Dr. DL1: Darl 5G 19
Richard Ct. DL1: Darl 5H 15
Richard Pease Ho.
  DL3: Darl 1F 19
Richardson Av. DL14: Bish A ..5F 3
Richardson Wlk.
  DL1: Darl 3G 11
Richard Ter. DL14: Bish A ...5C 4
Richmond Av. DL14: Bish A ...3G 3

Richmond Cl.—Stag La.

Richmond Cl. DL3: Darl 4C **14**
DL4: Shil 3D **8**
Richmond Rd. DL2: Croft T . . .6B **24**
Richmond Way DL1: Darl 4D **20**
Ricknall Av. DL5: Newt A 1G **13**
Ricknall La. DL5: Ayc 6H **11**
Ridgeway DL3: Darl 2G **15**
DL5: Newt A 1E **13**
Ridgewood Cl. DL1: Darl 5D **20**
Ridsdale St. DL1: Darl 2A **20**
Ringway Gro. DL2: Midd G . . .3C **22**
Ripon Dr. DL1: Darl 4A **20**
Rise, The DL3: Darl 3E **19**
RISE CARR **3G 15**
Ritson Rd. DL5: Newt A 5E **11**
Riverbank Trad. Est.
DL1: Darl 5H **15**
Rivergarth DL1: Haugh S 3E **17**
Rivermead Av.
DL1: Haugh S 3E **17**
Riverside DL14: Bish A 3B **4**
Riverside Dr. DL1: Gt Bur 4E **17**
Riverside Way
DL1: Haugh S 4B **16**
River Vw. Ind. Est.
DL1: Darl 5B **16**
River Wlk. DL14: W Auc 1C **6**
Roberts Wlk. *DL1: Darl 2A 20*
(off Carlton St.)
Robson Rd. DL14: W Auc 3B **6**
Robson St. DL4: Shil 1E **9**
Rochdale St. DL14: Even 5A **6**
Rochester Cl. DL14: Ether D . . .3E **3**
Rochester Way
DL1: Haugh S 5D **16**
Roche Wlk. DL3: Darl 4B **14**
Rockcliffe Ct. DL2: Hur P 5E **25**
Rockcliffe Ho. DL1: Darl 4B **20**
Rocket St. DL1: Darl 2A **20**
Rockingham Dr.
DL14: Ether D 3E **3**
Rockingham St. DL1: Darl 3H **19**
Rockwell Av. DL1: Haugh S . . .4C **16**
Rockwell Ho. DL1: Haugh S . . .4B **16**
Rodney Wlk. DL14: Coun 1F **5**
Roker Cl. DL1: Darl 6D **16**
Romaldkirk Wlk. DL1: Darl . . .4B **20**
Roman Rd. DL2: Midd G 5B **22**
Roman Way DL2: Midd G 5B **22**
Romanway Ind. Est.
DL14: Bish A 6G **3**
Rookhope Gro. DL14: Bish A . . .4E **3**
Rookwood Hunt
DL5: Newt A 3B **10**
Ropemoor Way
DL5: Newt A 1E **11**
Ropner Gdns. DL2: Midd G . . .6C **22**
Rosebay Ct. DL3: Darl 6F **15**
Roseberry Ter. DL4: Shil 1E **9**
Rosebery St. DL3: Darl 6F **15**
Rose Cotts. DL4: Shil 1D **8**
Rosedale Cres. DL3: Darl 5C **14**
DL4: Shil 2F **9**
Rose La. DL1: Haugh S 4D **16**
Rosemary Ct. DL1: Darl 4B **20**
Rosemount Ct. DL14: Bish A . . .4B **4**
Rosemount Rd. DL14: Bish A . . .4B **4**
Roslyn St. DL1: Darl 3H **19**
Ross Wlk. DL5: Newt A 5H **11**
Ross Way DL1: Haugh S 2D **16**
Rotary Way DL3: Darl 2C **14**
Rothbury Dr. DL3: Darl 4C **14**
Roundhill Cl. DL2: Hurw 4F **25**
Roundhill Rd.
DL2: Hur M, Hurw 6B **20**
Rowan Av. DL4: Shil 2F **9**
Rowan Ct. DL3: Darl 2D **18**
Rowan Pl. DL5: Newt A 5D **10**
Roxby Moor Av. DL1: Darl 4C **20**
Royal George Cl. DL4: Shil 4E **9**
Royal Oak Yd. DL3: Darl 1G **19**
Ruby St. DL3: Darl 3H **15**
DL4: Shil 2D **8**
Ruddock Av. DL14: Bish A 4G **3**
Rudland Way DL14: H Eth 5B **2**
Rufus Grn. Nth.
DL5: Newt A 3H **11**
Rufus Grn. Sth.
DL5: Newt A 3H **11**
Runnymede Ct. DL14: Bish A . . .1A **4**
Rush Pk. DL14: Bish A 3E **3**
Rushyford Ct. DL5: Newt A 3F **11**
Ruskin Av. DL4: Shil 2D **8**
Ruskin Rd. DL1: Darl 5H **19**
Russell Ct. DL5: Newt A 3C **10**
Russell St. DL1: Darl 1H **19**
DL14: Bish A 1H **3**
Rustland Dr. DL3: Darl 3E **19**
Rutland Av. DL14: Bish A 3H **3**
Rutland St. DL14: Leeh 1H **5**
Rydal Gro. DL14: W Auc 2A **6**
Rydal Rd. DL1: Darl 3A **20**
Ryder Ct. DL5: Newt A 1E **11**
Rye Hill DL3: Darl 5E **15**
Rylstone Cl. DL5: Newt A 3D **10**
Rymers Ct. DL1: Haugh S 4C **16**

S

SADBERGE **2H 17**
Saddler La. DL14: Even 6B **6**
Saddler St. DL14: Bish A 1H **3**
Saddlery, The DL5: Newt A . . .3B **10**
St Aidan's Wlk.
DL5: Newt A 3H **11**
DL14: Bish A 4A **4**
St Alban's Grn.
DL1: Haugh S 4E **17**
St Andrew's Cl.
DL1: Haugh S 5C **16**
DL5: Ayc 4G **13**
St Andrew's Crest
DL14: Bish A 2A **4**
St Andrew's Rd.
DL14: Bish A 4H **3**
(not continuous)
St Andrews St. DL1: Darl 4H **15**
St Andrew's Ter.
DL14: Bish A 2A **4**
St Andrews Way
DL5: Newt A 4F **13**
St Annes Gdns.
DL2: Midd G 5C **22**
St Augustines Ct. DL3: Darl . . .2G **19**
St Augustines Way
DL3: Darl 1G **19**
St Barbara's Wlk.
DL5: Newt A 3H **11**
St Chad's Cl. DL14: Bish A 4B **4**
St Cuthbert's Av. DL14: H Eth . . .6B **2**
St Cuthberts Pl. DL3: Darl 1F **19**
St Cuthberts Wlk.
DL14: Bish A 3A **4**
St Cuthberts Way DL1: Darl . . .1H **19**
DL5: Newt A 5F **11**
St David's Grn.
DL1: Haugh S 4E **17**
St Elizabeths Cl.
DL5: Newt A 1G **11**
St Georges Ga.
DL2: Midd G 2A **22**
St Giles Cl. DL3: Darl 2B **18**
St Godrics Rd. DL5: Newt A . . .5E **11**
ST HELEN AUCKLAND **1D 6**
St Helens Ind. Est.
DL14: St H 1E **7**
St Hildas Flats *DL1: Darl 1H 19*
(off Borough Rd.)
St Hild Cl. DL3: Darl 2C **18**
St John's Cres. DL1: Darl 2A **20**
St John's Pl. DL1: Darl 2A **20**
St John's Rd. DL4: Shil 3E **9**
St John's Wlk. DL14: Esc 1D **2**
St Luke's Cl. DL14: Bish A 5F **3**
St Margarets Cl.
DL2: Midd G 5C **22**
St Mark's Ct. DL14: Coun G 4D **4**
St Marys Cl. DL14: Bish A 4G **3**
St Michael's Cres.
DL5: Heigh 6A **12**
St Nicholas Ind. Est.
DL1: Darl 5B **16**
St Ninian's Cl. DL3: Darl 2B **18**
St Oswald's Cl. DL14: Bish A . . .3B **4**
St Oswald's Ct.
DL5: Newt A 4H **11**
St Oswald's Wlk.
DL5: Newt A 3H **11**
St Paul's Pl. DL1: Darl 4H **15**
St Pauls Ter. DL1: Darl 4H **15**
DL4: Shil 1E **9**
ST TERESA'S HOSPICE 1F 19
St Wilfrid's Wlk.
DL14: Bish A 4B **4**
(not continuous)
Salisbury Pl. DL2: Midd G 4B **22**
DL14: Bish A 2A **4**
Salisbury Ter. DL3: Darl 5G **15**
DL4: Shil 2D **8**
Salters Av. DL1: Haugh S 5C **16**
Salters Cl. DL1: Haugh S 3B **16**
Saltersgate Rd. DL1: Darl 2A **16**
Salters La. DL1: Darl 1A **16**
(Glebe Rd.)
DL1: Darl 4D **20**
(Yarm Rd.)
Salters La. Nth. DL1: Darl 2A **16**
Salters La. Sth.
DL1: Haugh S 3B **16**
Salt Yd. DL3: Darl 1G **19**
Salutation Rd. DL3: Darl 3B **18**
Sampson Pl. DL5: Newt A 3E **11**
Sanderson Cl. DL5: Newt A . . .3F **11**
Sanderson Rd. DL2: Hurw 4G **25**
Sanderson St. DL1: Darl 1H **19**
Sandown Dr. DL5: Newt A 1G **11**
Sandringham Ct. DL3: Darl . . .1B **18**
Sans Pareil Sq. DL3: Darl 4D **14**
Sawley Cl. DL3: Darl 4A **14**
Saxon Ct. DL14: Bish A 1G **3**
Saxon Grn. DL14: Esc 1D **2**
Scargill DL1: Darl 3B **20**
Scargill Ct. DL1: Darl 3B **20**
Scarth St. DL3: Darl 2F **19**
Scholars Pk. DL3: Darl 1F **19**
Scholar's Path
DL5: Newt A 4C **10**
SCHOOL AYCLIFFE **2B 12**
School Aycliffe La.
DL5: Sch A 3A **12**
School St. DL3: Darl 4D **14**
Scira Ct. DL1: Haugh S 4A **16**
Scott Pl. DL5: Newt A 3E **11**
Scott Rd. DL14: Bish A 5H **3**
Scotts Ter. DL3: Darl 3H **15**
Scott St. DL4: Shil 3D **8**
Secker Pl. DL5: Newt A 4H **11**
Sedgwick St. DL3: Darl 5F **15**
Selbourne Ter. DL3: Darl 6G **15**
Selby Cl. DL14: St H 1D **6**
Selby Cres. DL3: Darl 4B **14**
Selset Cl. DL1: Darl 4B **20**
Senhouse Rd. DL1: Darl 3E **21**
Seton Wlk. DL5: Newt A 6G **11**
Severn Way DL1: Darl 5H **19**
Seymour St. DL14: Bish A 4H **3**
Shafto Way DL5: Newt A 4G **11**
Shakespeare Rd. DL1: Darl . . .4H **19**
Shannon Lea DL2: Midd G 3D **22**
Shannon Way DL1: Darl 5G **19**
Sharp Rd. DL5: Newt A 5F **11**
Shawbrow Vw. DL3: Darl 1A **18**
DL14: Bish A 5H **3**
Shearwater Av. DL1: Darl 1C **20**
Shelly Rd. DL1: Darl 6B **16**
Sheppards Cft. DL5: Sch A 1B **12**
Sheraton Cl. DL5: Newt A 5G **11**
Sheraton Rd. DL5: Newt A 5F **11**
Sheraton St. DL3: Darl 4G **15**
Sherborne Cl. DL3: Darl 5A **14**
Sherborne Ho. DL3: Darl 5A **14**
Shetland Dr. DL1: Haugh S . . .2C **16**
Shield Wlk. DL5: Newt A 4G **11**
SHILDON **2F 9**
Shildon By-Pass DL4: Shil 3B **8**
Shildon Ct. DL4: Shil 3E **9**
Shildon Ind. Est. DL4: Shil 3E **9**
Shildon Leisure Cen. 1F 9
Shildon Rd. DL5: Redw 6F **9**
Shildon Station (Rail) **3F 9**
Shildon St. DL1: Darl 4H **15**
Shipley Gro. DL14: Bish A 4F **3**
Shirley Cl. DL14: Even 5B **6**
Shirley Ter. DL14: Even 5A **6**
Shorthorn La. DL3: Darl 3C **14**
Short St. DL14: Bish A 4H **3**
Shutts Ct. DL3: Darl 1G **19**
Sid Chaplin Dr.
DL5: Newt A 3E **11**
Sildale Cl. DL3: Darl 5F **15**
Silkin Way DL5: Newt A 5E **11**
Silverdale Pl. DL5: Newt A 4C **10**
Silver Pl. DL1: Darl 2A **20**
Simpasture Ct. DL5: Newt A . . .6E **11**
Simpasture Ga.
DL5: Newt A 6E **11**
Simpson Av. DL14: St H 6E **3**
Simpson Rd. DL14: W Auc 3B **6**
Sir E.D. Walker Homes
DL3: Darl 3D **18**
Skeeby Rd. DL1: Darl 3A **20**
Skeldale Gro. DL3: Darl 5F **15**
SKERNE PARK **5G 19**
Skerne Rd. DL5: Newt A 1G **13**
Skerningham Av. DL3: Darl . . .3B **14**
Skerries Wlk.
DL1: Haugh S 2C **16**
Skinnergate DL3: Darl 2G **19**
Skipton Cl. DL5: Newt A 4D **10**
Skipton Gro. DL14: Bish A 3G **3**
Skipton Moor Cl. DL1: Darl . . .4C **20**
Skirlaw Rd. DL5: Newt A 5G **11**
Skye Wlk. DL1: Haugh S 2C **16**
Smithfield Rd. DL1: Darl 3H **19**
Smith Wlk. DL5: Newt A 4G **11**
Smythsons Cl. DL5: Sch A 1B **12**
Snackgate La. DL5: Heigh 6B **12**
Snipe La. DL1: Darl 5G **19**
DL2: Darl 5F **19**
Snowdrop Way
DL14: Ether D 3E **3**
Soho Cotts. DL4: Shil 3E **9**
Soho St. DL4: Shil 3E **9**
Somerset Gro. DL1: Darl 5B **16**
Somerville Ct. DL1: Darl 3A **16**
Sorrell Wynd DL5: Newt A 1F **11**
Southampton St. DL1: Darl . . .5H **15**
Sth. Arden St. DL1: Darl 2G **19**
South Bank DL3: Darl 1F **19**
SOUTH CHURCH **4B 4**
Sth. Church Ent. Pk.
DL14: Bish A 4B **4**
Sth. Church Rd.
DL14: Bish A 1A **4**
Southcliffe *DL14: Bish A 5B 4*
(off Milford Mdw.)
South Cotts. DL5: Sch A 1C **12**
Southend Av. DL3: Darl 3F **19**
Southend Pl. DL3: Darl 2F **19**
Southfield Cl. DL2: Hurw 4G **25**
Southfield Dr. DL14: Toft H 6A **2**
Southgate St. DL14: Bish A 2A **4**
Southgrove DL5: Ayc 4H **13**
Southland Gdns. DL4: Shil 1D **8**
Southmoor Cl. DL1: Darl 4C **20**
South Pde. DL2: Croft T 5B **24**
South Rd. DL14: H Eth 6A **2**
South Row DL5: Ayc 4G **13**
DL14: Eld 5E **5**
South Side DL5: Middr 2A **10**
South St. DL3: Darl 5G **15**
DL4: Shil 3D **8**
South Ter. DL1: Darl 2G **19**
DL4: Shil 3A **8**
DL14: Bish A 1A **4**
South Vw. DL2: Sadb 2H **17**
DL4: Shil 1E **9**
DL5: Heigh 6B **12**
DL14: Bish A 2A **4**
DL14: Coun 1F **5**
DL14: Even 6A **6**
Southwell Grn.
DL1: Haugh S 5D **16**
Spa Bank DL2: Croft T 6B **24**
Sparrow Hall Dr.
DL1: Haugh S 2B **16**
Speedwell Cl. DL1: Darl 2B **20**
Spencely St. DL4: Shil 1D **8**
Spencer Gro. DL1: Darl 4B **20**
Spencer St. DL14: Eld L 5D **4**
Spinney, The DL2: Midd G 3E **23**
DL3: Darl 5E **19**
DL5: Newt A 1F **11**
Spooner Cl. DL5: Newt A 2D **10**
Spout La. DL4: Shil 3F **9**
Spring Ct. DL3: Darl 4D **14**
SPRINGFIELD **3B 16**
Springfield Rd.
DL1: Haugh S 3B **16**
Springfields DL5: Sch A 1B **12**
SPRING GARDENS **1A 6**
Spring Hill DL3: Darl 3G **15**
Spring Rd. DL5: Newt A 3E **13**
Springwell Ter.
DL1: Haugh S 4B **16**
Spruce Ct. DL4: Shil 3F **9**
Spruce Gro. DL3: Darl 2D **18**
Square, The DL2: Midd G 3B **22**
DL14: St H 1D **6**
Squires Ct. DL3: Darl 6D **14**
Stag La. DL5: Newt A 1G **11**